THYESTES

Thomas Henning, Chris Ryan, Simon Stone & Mark Winter
after Seneca

CURRENCY PRESS
SYDNEY

CURRENCY PLAYS

First published in 2012
by Currency Press Pty Ltd,
PO Box 2287, Strawberry Hills, NSW, 2012, Australia
enquiries@currency.com.au
www.currency.com.au
in association with Belvoir, Sydney.

Copyright © Thomas Henning, Chris Ryan, Simon Stone, Mark Winter, 2011.

COPYING FOR EDUCATIONAL PURPOSES
The Australian *Copyright Act 1968* (Act) allows a maximum of one chapter or 10% of this book, whichever is the greater, to be copied by any educational institution for its educational purposes provided that that educational institution (or the body that administers it) has given a remuneration notice to Copyright Agency Limited (CAL) under the Act.

For details of the CAL licence for educational institutions contact CAL, Level 15/233 Castlereagh Street, Sydney, NSW, 2000, Australia; tel: within Australia 1800 066 844 toll free; outside Australia 61 2 9394 7600; fax: 61 2 9394 7601; email: info@copyright.com.au

COPYING FOR OTHER PURPOSES
Except as permitted under the Act, for example a fair dealing for the purposes of study, research, criticism or review, no part of this book may be reproduced, stored in a retrieval system, or transmitted in any form or by any means without prior written permission. All enquiries should be made to the publisher at the address above.

Any performance or public reading of *Thyestes* is forbidden unless a licence has been received from the authors or the authors' agent. The purchase of this book in no way gives the purchaser the right to perform the play in public, whether by means of a staged production or a reading. All applications for public performance should be addressed to the authors c/- Currency Press.

NATIONAL LIBRARY OF AUSTRALIA CIP DATA

Title:	Thyestes / co-written by Thomas Henning ... [et al.]
ISBN:	9780868199276 (pbk.)
Series:	Current theatre series.
Notes:	'Based on the original by Seneca the Younger written in the 1st century AD'.
Subjects:	Seneca, Lucius Annaeus, ca. 4 B.C.–65 A.D. Thyestes.
	Thyestes (Greek mythology)–Drama.
	Thyestes (Greek mythology) in literature.
Other Authors/Contributors:	
	Henning, Thomas William.

Dewey Number: A822.4

Typeset by Dean Nottle for Currency Press.
Printed by Ligare Pty Ltd, Riverwood, NSW.
Cover design by Tim Kliendienst, Alphabet Studio.

Contents

THYESTES

   Act One   1

   Act Two   23

Theatre Program at the end of the playtext

ACKNOWLEDGMENTS

The authors would like to thank our dramaturg Anne-Louise Sarks and the creatives, Stefan Gregory, Govin Ruben and Claude Marcos, for their invaluable contribution to the development of this script. We would also like to acknowledge Michael Kantor, Stephen Armstrong, Benedict Hardie, Carl Nilsson-Polias, Tahni Froudist and everyone at The Hayloft Project and Malthouse Theatre for their unending support of both the work and the artists involved.

Thyestes was first produced by The Hayloft Project at the Malthouse, Melbourne, as a Malthouse Theatre commission, on 16 September 2010, with the following cast:

THYESTES	Thomas Henning
ATREUS	Mark Winter
CHRYSIPPUS / AEROPE / AEGISTHUS / PELOPIA	Chris Ryan

Director, Simon Stone
Set & Costume Designer, Claude Marcos
Lighting Designer, Govin Ruben
Composer & Sound Designer, Stefan Gregory
Dramaturg, Anne-Louise Sarks

CHARACTERS

THYESTES
CHRYSIPPUS
ATREUS
AEROPE
AEGISTHUS
PELOPIA

AUTHOR'S NOTE

Thyestes was written by the actors and myself with the aim to improvise significantly on the text each night. Therefore this script represents an indicative example of an average night's performance and not anything definitive.

All roles, male and female, are played by men. The roles of Chrysippus, Aerope, Aegisthus and Pelopia are played by a single actor. The actors playing Thyestes and Atreus play only one role each.

In the second act, the scenes move backwards through time, hence the reverse order of scene numbering.

At the beginning of each scene there is a section of text in inverted commas. This text represents a projected surtitle that is shown to the audience before each scene.

Simon Stone

ACT ONE

SCENE ONE

SURTITLE: *'Ancient Greece, Kingdom of Pisa. King Pelops has declared his bastard child, Chrysippus, heir to the throne. Enraged, his wife, Queen Hippodamia, convinces her sons, Atreus and Thyestes, to kill their half-brother Chrysippus.'*

Curtain up. We discover an empty white room with three young men in it. They're sharing a bottle of red wine. CHRYSIPPUS *is in the middle of telling* ATREUS *and* THYESTES *a story.* ATREUS *is texting on his phone.*

CHRYSIPPUS: So we've organised to meet at Miami airport, right?
THYESTES: Right.
CHRYSIPPUS: And the day comes around and I'm standing there in the arrivals section, you know where all the families wait?
THYESTES: Yeah, yeah, and they've got those big glass windows.
CHRYSIPPUS: That's it, they've got the big glass windows. That's where I was. And I'm looking up at the screen and it's saying that her plane has landed about two hours ago. And there's no sign of her. So I'm like, that's weird.
THYESTES: Yeah.
CHRYSIPPUS: You know. But maybe she's got caught up in some customs area and I'll see her on the other side.
THYESTES: Yeah, yeah.
CHRYSIPPUS: So I just go to our departure gate. We've got like a five-hour layover.
THYESTES: Get to do any duty free?
CHRYSIPPUS: No. No duty free.
THYESTES: Oh.
CHRYSIPPUS: So I'm waiting there for ages and—

ATREUS' *phone receives a text message.*

ATREUS: Sorry, man.
CHRYSIPPUS: And um... at this stage she's still not there and I'm like putting announcements all over the Miami airport. Going, please

come to this gate. And that kind of thing. And by this time everyone's on the plane, right?
THYESTES: Yeah.
CHRYSIPPUS: I'm the only one left. So I go up to the desk. And I go, excuse me but I need you to check your passenger list for me.
THYESTES: They can't give that kind of information out.
CHRYSIPPUS: That's what they said. They said, they can't give that kind of information out. And I said, please, my girlfriend's meant to be on that plane.
THYESTES: Girlfriend?
CHRYSIPPUS: Yeah. We talked about it in Costa Rica and decided.
THYESTES: That's great, man.
CHRYSIPPUS: Thanks. Anyway.

    ATREUS *receives two text messages in quick succession.*

ATREUS: Whoa. Double.
CHRYSIPPUS: So they do me the favour and they check their passenger list. And they say, sorry sir, but there's no-one by that name on this flight.
THYESTES: Really?
CHRYSIPPUS: Yeah, I know. So I just have to get on this plane, no idea what's going on.
THYESTES: Where was it going?
CHRYSIPPUS: Guatemala City.
THYESTES: Right.
CHRYSIPPUS: Yeah, so I'm kind of like sitting on the plane in this daze thinking, where is she, what the hell is going on? And then I hear this voice talking to me in Spanish and I turn around and I'm like, 'what?' And this guy goes, [*putting on an American voice*] 'Oh I'm sorry'. Turns out this guy's American.
THYESTES: Yeah, right.
CHRYSIPPUS: Anyway—
ATREUS: What's this?
THYESTES: Trip to Guatemala.
ATREUS: Oh.
CHRYSIPPUS: Yeah. So he hears my voice and he says, what are you doing here? And I said, well I was meant to meet my girlfriend. And

ACT ONE 3

he's like, well where is she and I say she didn't turn up, I don't know what's happened and then he goes, have you been to Guatemala City before and I say no and he's like, it's a pretty dangerous place if you don't know your way around, I start to freak out and then he goes, [*putting on the American voice*] 'How's your Spanish?' [*Explaining to* ATREUS, *who is looking at him strangely*] This guy's American.

ATREUS: Right.

CHRYSIPPUS: And I said I don't speak any Spanish, she speaks all the Spanish. Anyway, it turns out this guy is a priest.

THYESTES: Really?

CHRYSIPPUS: And the plane lands. And I go through customs and this guy, this priest, is waiting for me at the baggage carousel.

THYESTES: Right.

ATREUS: Whoa.

CHRYSIPPUS: Yeah. No [*laughing*] he's waiting there and he comes up to me and says are you okay, you don't know your way around, maybe I can find a place for you to stay. And I'm like that'd be great. And we get in this cab. And we're—

ATREUS: Whoa.

CHRYSIPPUS: No, it's not like that, he's a good guy this guy.

ATREUS: They always are good guys at first.

CHRYSIPPUS: So we get in this cab and we go to this hotel.

ATREUS: Whoa.

CHRYSIPPUS: And get this, there's this priest conference going on.

ATREUS: Shit. Oh, shit.

CHRYSIPPUS: All the priests from Central and South America have descended on Guatemala City for this conference.

ATREUS: That's the scariest thing I've ever heard.

CHRYSIPPUS: It was fine. So I just hung out at this priest conference.

THYESTES: Yeah, right. Was that weird?

CHRYSIPPUS: No, it was good. I was kind of naïve though.

ATREUS: Yes you were.

CHRYSIPPUS: No, I mean about the language. Like, when I first got there and I went through customs, they were like *'Passaporte'* and I'm like, what? I don't even know the word for 'what'.

ATREUS: *Que*.

CHRYSIPPUS: Yeah, that's it. *Que*.
ATREUS: *Que*. *Que*.
CHRYSIPPUS: Yeah, that's it. And that's what they're doing. They're going, '*Que, que*'. 'Cause I'm saying English, English. I didn't even know the word for English.
ATREUS: *Inglais*.
CHRYSIPPUS: Yeah, I know.
ATREUS: You just said you didn't know.
CHRYSIPPUS: Yeah but I do now.
ATREUS: Want to know how I know?
CHRYSIPPUS: How?
ATREUS: CAE.
CHRYSIPPUS: What's CAE?
ATREUS: Centre for Adult Education.
CHRYSIPPUS: You go to Adult Education?
ATREUS: They've got great courses, man, you should check it out. I did two days of Spanish then I switched to woodwork.
THYESTES: I didn't know that.
ATREUS: Well, I'm a mysterious man.
THYESTES: Yes, you are. Yes, you are.
CHRYSIPPUS: You certainly are.
THYESTES: So what happened? You're at this priest conference?
CHRYSIPPUS: Yeah, and then that ended after a couple of days. And the American priest, he goes back to Peru because he's some kind of missionary or something. And then the others, the ones who were left, the Guatemalan ones, they didn't know who the fuck I was. So I just walked off.
THYESTES: Where'd you go?
CHRYSIPPUS: I just drifted around Guatemala City.

He moves over to THYESTES *to refill his wineglass.*

THYESTES: What's it like?
CHRYSIPPUS: It's really full-on.
THYESTES: Yeah?
CHRYSIPPUS: Yeah. There's all these guys that just stand on street corners with sawn-off shotguns. Because all the police over there are corrupt. So everyone has to hire their own private security. And

they're just random dudes, not in security uniforms or anything, just random dudes in shorts and singlets holding sawn-off shotguns.

THYESTES: Sunglasses and shit?

CHRYSIPPUS: Yeah, yeah, yeah. At first you think, everyone's got guns here.

THYESTES: Or there's a war going on.

CHRYSIPPUS: Yeah, but then you realise—

THYESTES: It's just security.

CHRYSIPPUS: Yeah.

THYESTES: That's crazy.

CHRYSIPPUS: I saw this other guy, not one of the security guys, just this guy, I saw him kill a dog with a brick.

THYESTES: Like a stray dog?

CHRYSIPPUS: Yeah.

THYESTES: Was he planning to eat it or something?

CHRYSIPPUS: Oh no. They're good for food there. The impression I got was that the dog had done something the guy didn't like. And he was kind of taking his revenge.

THYESTES: Brutal revenge.

ATREUS has made his way over to the other two.

CHRYSIPPUS: And everyone else is standing around like it's just another day in Guatemala City. Eventually I met this other guy who spoke a bit of English. He told me about this cheap hotel just around the corner. So I go there, and check in, right, walk into the room, flick on the telly and guess what it is? 'Water Rats'. But in Spanish. It's dubbed. There's Colin Friels, zooming around Sydney Harbour going '*Arriba, arriba*' or some shit. Friels has got his own Spanish voice. It's bit like that show, remember that show 'Monkey Magic'? Dubbed from Chinese—

ATREUS is pretending to be one of the characters in 'Monkey Magic'.

Yeah, yeah, that's right, that's right, then he jumps on the cloud. Yeah, it's the same as that except it's Colin—

ATREUS: Hey, you know the Buddha from 'Monkey Magic'?

CHRYSIPPUS: Tripitaka.

ATREUS: Yeah. Was that a dude or a chick?

THYESTES: I think it was a woman but she was playing a guy. Which made her kind of androgynous.
ATREUS: Yeah, 'cause I always wanted to fuck the Buddha from 'Monkey Magic' but I could never work it out.
CHRYSIPPUS: I think it was a guy.
ATREUS: It's like that middle sister from Hanson.
CHRYSIPPUS: Hanson was a boy band.
ATREUS: I know. I know. But I thought the middle sister was just, you know, and I really wanted to fuck her.
CHRYSIPPUS: Middle brother.
ATREUS: Middle brother. Yeah. There's thousands of us online. Lot of people wanted to fuck the middle sister from Hanson.
CHRYSIPPUS: Middle brother.
ATREUS: Yeah.
CHRYSIPPUS: And even if it was a girl, she was like eight years old man.
ATREUS: Yeah, but once you're in the public sphere, you know, it changes things.
CHRYSIPPUS: Jesus.
THYESTES: Hey, what happened to your girlfriend?
ATREUS: Girlfriend?
THYESTES: Yeah, they hooked up in Costa Rica. That's why he was in Guatemala.
ATREUS: Heeeeey. Way to go, man.
CHRYSIPPUS: Thanks, man.
ATREUS: Alright.
THYESTES: Did you meet up with her or what?
CHRYSIPPUS: I emailed her and I was like, where are you? And she wrote back, she was meant to be coming in October. Not September.
ATREUS: You missed her by a fucking month?
CHRYSIPPUS: Well, I had the right day of the month.
ATREUS: That is a huge fucking mix-up man. A whole fucking month.
THYESTES: What, did you chase her down?
CHRYSIPPUS: I wrote back to her and said, what's your cousin's address, 'cause that's where we were going to stay, I thought maybe I could just hang out there till she came. And, uh, I never heard from her again.
THYESTES: Man. That sucks.

ACT ONE 7

CHRYSIPPUS: Yeah. Still haven't heard from her. She was nice.
ATREUS: Hey, look, come on. Young buck like you. Plenty of fish in the sea.
THYESTES: Plenty of fish.

CHRYSIPPUS *proposes a toast.*

CHRYSIPPUS: To the fish. In the sea.

They join him.

ATREUS: I think I've worked out what we're getting this guy for Christmas. A fucking calendar, you fucking retard, that's a whole fucking month you fucked up there.
CHRYSIPPUS: I once went out with this other girl, she tried to organise my life.

He sighs.

ATREUS: I feel like I should hug you, man.

He hugs him.

CHRYSIPPUS: She just wasn't the one, I guess.
ATREUS: Wasn't the one.
CHRYSIPPUS: Wasn't the one. And that's what I want now, I want the one. I'm sick of messing around.
ATREUS: It's all cycles, isn't it? I met this great chick.
THYESTES: Oh, yeah?
ATREUS: Yeah, this one's different, you know. She's beautiful. She's funny. She's smart.
CHRYSIPPUS: The package.
ATREUS: That's right. She's changed my life, man.

THYESTES *is laughing.*

What?
THYESTES: What?
ATREUS: Why are you laughing?
THYESTES: It's funny.
ATREUS: What's funny about it? I'm not joking.
THYESTES: Sorry.
ATREUS: Are you making fun of me?
THYESTES: No, man.
ATREUS: What are you trying to say? Huh?

THYESTES: It's okay, man.

An awkward pause.

CHRYSIPPUS: Hey. If it's not on, it's not on.

ATREUS: It's funny you should say that. I had a blood test the other week. Came back negative.

CHRYSIPPUS: No way.

ATREUS: I know.

THYESTES: That's crazy.

ATREUS: I know.

CHRYSIPPUS: You?

ATREUS: I'm as surprised as you guys are. Not even herpes.

CHRYSIPPUS: Even I've got herpes.

ATREUS: What?

CHRYSIPPUS: Cold sores. Cold sores are a strain of herpes. I get cold sores all the time. It's not the vicious genital type.

ATREUS: Right.

THYESTES: [*to* ATREUS] Are you sure they gave you the right results? They didn't accidently swap them with a monk's?

ATREUS *pulls the test results out of his pocket.*

ATREUS: Take a look. My name.

CHRYSIPPUS: You carry your test results round in your pocket?

ATREUS: Of course I do. Everyone should in this day and age. Cut out the guesswork. It's like crossing a border. You need your papers. Look. My name. My results. Negative all down the column.

CHRYSIPPUS: Congratulations.

ATREUS: We've been having candlelit dinners.

THYESTES: Who?

ATREUS: Me and this new girl. Seriously. It's all romantic and shit. We've been taking those carriage rides with the horses where they put a blanket on your lap. Went to the opera.

CHRYSIPPUS: What?

THYESTES: You're kidding.

ATREUS: I did. I went to the opera.

CHRYSIPPUS: Doesn't that go for like four hours?

ATREUS: It went for fucking ages. The thing just kept going and going and going. I mean who has the time?

CHRYSIPPUS: I hear it's just all singing. Nothing else. No talking.
THYESTES: Did you fall asleep?
ATREUS: I didn't actually. I came prepared. I kind of knew what I was in for so I brought my iPod and put the headphones up the sleeve of my jacket. Then I sort of tucked them into my ear—

He makes the gesture of pretending to lean on his hand while listening to his iPod.

CHRYSIPPUS: What were you listening to on your iPod?
ATREUS: BBC wildlife podcast.
CHRYSIPPUS: So you had the opera in one ear and BBC wildlife in the other?
ATREUS: It was great man. Surround sound.
THYESTES: Did she notice?
ATREUS: No, she was up on the stage.
CHRYSIPPUS: On the stage?
ATREUS: Yeah. She's an opera singer.
CHRYSIPPUS: What the fuck?
THYESTES: Where the fuck did you meet an opera singer?
ATREUS: I met her in a fucking bar, where do you think I'd meet an opera singer? Yeah, it was one of those modern interpretations of an opera. I don't know what it was called. Like *Don Giogiggy* or something.
CHRYSIPPUS: I'm pretty sure it wasn't called *Don Giogiggy*.
ATREUS: Well, whatever it was called there were no horns or anything. No breastplates or spears. But she looked astonishing up there. She looked really beautiful under all those lights.
CHRYSIPPUS: Did you see that? When he said astonishing he went like this. [*He puts his hands into a breast-cupping shape.*] Astonishing. Massive tits?
ATREUS: You really asking me that?
CHRYSIPPUS: Just between the fellas.
ATREUS: Well, let me see if I can describe this to you. You might need to open up your mind a few notches. The only way I can really describe it to you is, it's like seeing the face of God on a woman's chest.
CHRYSIPPUS: God has a beard man. [*He laughs.*] She's got hairy tits.
ATREUS: You don't understand, man. You don't understand. I do not expect you to get this but it's not that God. It's an old ancient woman god. It's primal. It brings tears to my eyes just to think about it.

CHRYSIPPUS: Those are some norgs.
ATREUS: Norgs?
CHRYSIPPUS: Yeah. Norgs.
ATREUS: The highlight of the opera was like three hours into this thing. This boy walks on with this huge black stallion.
CHRYSIPPUS: A real horse?
ATREUS: Yeah, a real horse. And they must have taken it for a run beforehand because this horse was like sweating up and foaming. I mean, I didn't get to see any swordfights but this thing was beautiful. And it just stands there for four or five minutes with this kid holding onto it and then it takes this massive steamer. And then they've got this other guy, it must be like Top Gun or something, he's waiting outside and he gets like a 'ten-four buddy, we got a steamer' and he comes in and he's got a broom and sweeps it up. That's his job. He just waits for his 'ten-four, we got a steamer'.
CHRYSIPPUS: Is that part of the show? Like every night? I wonder how they make that happen.
ATREUS: I think the horse just does it. It's a wild creature. It just does what it wants.
CHRYSIPPUS: You could give it like an enema before it goes on stage.
ATREUS: I think that'd be fairly unethical, man. And it didn't seem that important to the story. I don't think they needed the steamer.
CHRYSIPPUS: So what's this girl like in the old sack-a-roonie?
ATREUS: Sack-a-roonie?
CHRYSIPPUS: Yeah, it means—
ATREUS: I know what it means. Where the fuck do you come up with these phrases?
CHRYSIPPUS: Just between fellas, man.
ATREUS: Well, to tell you the truth, my dick has not gone an inch near her little slice of heaven.
THYESTES: What do you mean?
ATREUS: She fucks me.
THYESTES: What?
CHRYSIPPUS: No *comprende*.
ATREUS: She's got a strap-on. She pounds me like a goddamn woodpecker. It's unbelievable. It is all up in the prostate. I'm seeing things in fucking 3D. It's a whole new world. Like a magic eye puzzle. I'm

seeing through shit. You guys ever been fucked in the arse? Get on this train. Prostate. Prostate. Prostate. I cannot express this enough. A whole new world. You hear songs and shit. This girl is unbelievable. Get this. I make her an origami flower—
CHRYSIPPUS: Where the fuck did you learn to make an origami flower?
ATREUS: At the CAE. They offer it as an add-on. I make her an origami flower and she blows me in the lift.
CHRYSIPPUS: What?
ATREUS: I'm telling you, she's unbelievable.
CHRYSIPPUS: How did you make that happen?
ATREUS: I didn't do anything. She just did it.
CHRYSIPPUS: You didn't ask her?
ATREUS: What a woman. She just did it.
CHRYSIPPUS: She's an opera singer.
ATREUS: Yeah?
CHRYSIPPUS: Can you imagine?
ATREUS: What?
CHRYSIPPUS: The vocal cords.
ATREUS: What do you mean?
CHRYSIPPUS: Did she sing?
ATREUS: Of course she didn't sing. She had my dick in her mouth.
CHRYSIPPUS: Yeah, but I mean you still could. I mean— [*He holds an imaginary penis in his hand.*] I mean I don't know how big your dick is. [*He makes a larger penis with his hand and puts it in his mouth. He sings like an opera singer.*] Can you imagine the vibrations? The buzzing? [*He pretends to be receiving the opera singer's blow job.*] You should get her to do that.
ATREUS: Fuck yeah, man, I'm going to text that through to her.
CHRYSIPPUS: Hey, no, I wouldn't do that.
ATREUS: No no, you don't understand, man, she's up for this stuff. She'll probably bring a friend.
CHRYSIPPUS: This is the kind of girl I need to meet.
ATREUS: No, man, you're not ready for that. You need to start showing up on time first, not a month fucking early.

He texts on his phone.

CHRYSIPPUS: This is really nice wine. What is it, a sav blanc?

THYESTES: No, it's a red wine.
CHRYSIPPUS: Yeah. I always get that mixed up. Cab sav/sav blanc. Kind of like the pinot gris/pinot noir thing.
THYESTES: Hey, we should put some music on.
ATREUS: Actually my computer crashed and I've only got one playlist on my iPod and I've been listening to it over and over.
CHRYSIPPUS: Well we haven't heard it.
THYESTES: Yeah, some atmosphere.
ATREUS: I'd really rather not. I'd just prefer to talk.
CHRYSIPPUS: Come on, dude, let's have some beats.
ATREUS: I don't have 'beats' on my iPod.
THYESTES: Come on, man. Let's have some music.
ATREUS: Fine. Yeah. Alright. Yeah. Let's listen to some music. That'll be great.

> CHRYSIPPUS *turns to the iPod. His back is now to the brothers.* ATREUS *mouths 'fuck you' to* THYESTES.

CHRYSIPPUS: Thanks for having me round, guys. It's great to be here.
ATREUS: [*staring daggers at* THYESTES] No, it's good to have you here man.

> CHRYSIPPUS *selects a track. Roy Orbison's 'Anything You Want' starts playing.*

CHRYSIPPUS: Roy Orbison. Man. I love Roy Orbison.

> CHRYSIPPUS *sings along to the song.* THYESTES *and* ATREUS *share looks. Slowly,* THYESTES *stands up and walks a few steps away. He turns to look at* CHRYSIPPUS. *Both brothers stand and watch* CHRYSIPPUS, *his back to them and singing.* CHRYSIPPUS *doesn't hear* THYESTES *pull out a gun and cock it. The brothers look at each other. They look back to* CHRYSIPPUS.
>
> *Curtain.*

SCENE TWO

SURTITLE: *'King Pelops has exiled Atreus and Thyestes for murdering Chrysippus. After a year travelling from one kingdom to another, the brothers have settled in Mycenae. News arrives of their mother's suicide.'*

ACT ONE

Curtain up. THYESTES *and* ATREUS *are playing ping-pong. They share random conversation. This continues for quite some time. At one point the phone rings.* ATREUS *hangs it up without answering. When the first game is won, the loser is punished by standing blindfolded and topless against the wall while the winner takes three pot shots at him. A new game commences. More random conversation. The phone rings again. They ignore it and keep playing.*

Curtain.

SCENE THREE

SURTITLE: *'Following the death of King Eurystheus, Atreus and Thyestes have been crowned joint kings of Mycenae. They agree to alternate which of them sits on the throne from one year to the next. To celebrate their coronation, Atreus chooses a wife: Aerope, princess of Crete.'*

Curtain up. It is very early morning. A party has been going since lunchtime the day before. The Wu-Tang Clan's 'Gravel Pit' is playing loudly. ATREUS *is dancing with the wall.* AEROPE *is racking up lines of cocaine, occasionally taking a sip from a gin bottle and chasing it with a sip from a bottle of tonic water.* THYESTES *is reading a copy of Jean-Jacques Rousseau's 'The Social Contract'.* ATREUS *presses pause on the music.*

ATREUS: You know the thing I love about the Wu-Tang Clan is what the RZA said about the Wu-Tang Clan. He said that individually the members of the Wu-Tang Clan are just fingers. Weak. Breakable. But combined, they make a fist. Solid. Unbreakable. I love the Wu-Tang Clan. But now, for something completely different.

He puts on Rick Ross's 'Hustlin'. He stares at one of the ceiling lights without moving. When the song breaks, he dances wildly over AEROPE. *Just as suddenly he stops moving and stares at another ceiling light. Eventually he gives up and turns the track off.*

Man, my knees are really sore. Anyone else's knees really sore? I think maybe I should just duck down to the chemist. Anyone want a mission? We'll go to the chemist and get an icepack. And a cold-compressor pack. And maybe an icy pole. Anyone else feel like an icy pole? Because I could kill for an icy pole. Maybe a Frosty Fruit or something. Frosty Fruit? Man, it feels like love in the air. Because of you. People. Because you're my family. This one's for you.

He plays Mary J. Blige's 'A Family Affair'. He dances suggestively against the wall, slapping his arse in AEROPE's *direction.* AEROPE *woops. The dance gets sexier,* ATREUS *gyrating his groin towards her. He takes his t-shirt off. He undoes his belt. He drops to the floor and performs a series of half push-up/half commando-crawl movements, in time with the music, towards* AEROPE. *When he gets to her,* AEROPE *kisses his belly button. He pushes her away and gestures for money with his hand.* AEROPE *takes the fifty-dollar note she's been snorting cocaine with and puts it in his underpants. Her hand lingers there until he removes it and slaps it haughtily. He pulls her head into his belly and she starts to kiss up his body towards his face. A prolonged kiss, dancing together.* AEROPE *pushes him off her and gestures for* THYESTES *to call a taxi.* THYESTES *picks up the phone and rings.*

One more song, one more song then we can go. One more song. One more song then we can go. I need a Frosty Fruit and I really need a shirt.

He plays Ice Cube's 'You Can Do It'. He performs a monkey dance to it. AEROPE *tries to clothe him. Eventually she gets the t-shirt onto him. She begins to do up his belt. She checks to see whether* THYESTES *is looking. She puts her hand down* ATREUS' *pants and starts to jerk him off. This continues for a while until the phone rings in the background and she withdraws her hand and walks away.* ATREUS *falls to the floor.* THYESTES *answers the phone.*

That is so cruel.
THYESTES: Taxi's here.
ATREUS: You've just put two hours onto our departure time because I've got to tuck it into my belt now.
AEROPE: Come on.
ATREUS: I'm going as fast as I can. Hey, I've found your fifty dollars. I'll keep it.
AEROPE: Put your jacket on.

She puts it on him.

ACT ONE

ATREUS: Shit, where's my keys?

AEROPE: For fuck's sake, not again.

ATREUS: I can't find my keys.

AEROPE: Where did you last see them?

ATREUS: I don't know.

AEROPE: Go back through your movements, step by step.

ATREUS: I'm trying. I can't remember the last thirty-six hours. Sweetie, can you check my pockets for me?

AEROPE: For fuck's sake.

ATREUS: Just do the double check. Check my pockets.

AEROPE checks his pockets. She finds a ring box.

What is that? That's not my keys.

AEROPE: What is this?

ATREUS: I don't know, baby, open it up, take a look. [*She does.*] Whoa. Looks expensive.

AEROPE: Now? You chose now to do this?

ATREUS: Yeah, it feels like there's a lot of love in the—

AEROPE: Fuck you. This is not the time or place.

ATREUS: What do you mean?

AEROPE: We've been wasted for the past eight hours.

ATREUS: So? There's a lot of love in the—

AEROPE: Fuck you. Where's the romance? Where's the candle dinner?

ATREUS: We can go get some Nando's on the way if you want.

AEROPE: I don't want Nando's. I'm going to forget I ever saw this. It is quite nice.

ATREUS: Yeah.

AEROPE: I'm forgetting I've seen this. You can take it back and do this properly some other time. Where's the bended knee for starters?

ATREUS: Well, give me another go. Look, I'll—

He gets down on both knees.

AEROPE: It's bended knee. Not knees.

ATREUS: Don't tie me down with technicalities. You're my girl. Are you in or you out?

Curtain.

SCENE FOUR

SURTITLE: *'Years pass. Thyestes takes a wife and she bears him two sons and a daughter. During his years of reign Atreus' tyranny grows more and more horrific. Thyestes decides to depose Atreus and become sole King of Mycenae. He seduces Atreus' wife, Queen Aerope.'*

Curtain up. THYESTES' *children's bedroom. There is a tent on the floor, with a light on inside it.* ATREUS *is having a psychotic attack. He has forced his way into their bedroom and is trying to get into the tent.* THYESTES *is trying to stop him.* ATREUS *has a whisky bottle in his hand.* AEROPE *is standing distraught in the corner.*

ATREUS: The fucking cunt's locked me out.

THYESTES: Watch your language.

ATREUS: What are you standing in my way for? I've got to get in there and sort this out.

THYESTES: Come back outside. Let's finish dinner.

ATREUS: I've been fucking his missus and now he won't let me in.

THYESTES: Brother, you're at home. That's a tent. My kids are in there.

ATREUS: Your what?

THYESTES: I need you to take a step back.

ATREUS: Don't fucking tell me what to do. Nobody fucking tells me what to do. Get the fuck out of my way.

THYESTES: Come on, brother, calm down.

ATREUS: I am calm. I've got to talk to this cunt. Make him understand. We're in some serious shit here, bro.

THYESTES: We're at home and there's nothing to worry about.

ATREUS: No, I fucked his wife and he's never really liked me anyway and he knows way too much for us to let this lie. We got to sort it out.

THYESTES: You're drunk.

ATREUS: I'm not fucking drunk.

THYESTES: Why don't you just go to bed?

ATREUS: I'm going to shoot the fucking lock in. I'm going to talk to the cunt and if he doesn't seem amenable, you know what we got to do.

AEROPE: Honey, just go to bed.

ATREUS: Who's this bitch?

THYESTES: It's your wife.

ATREUS: Fucking sluts. I can't get the stench off me.
AEROPE: Honey.
ATREUS: Always a fucking headache. It's not serious. It's not serious it's not fucking serious and then you go and take it serious.

He backs AEROPE *up against a wall.*

I got a wife, I got to keep it together, I can't have you fucking my shit up. I am warning you. You're expendable. I can make you disappear. They'll be trawling the rivers for you and all they'll find is a bracelet, don't fucking tempt me.

He starts to attack her now. THYESTES *wrestles* ATREUS *to the ground.*

Get off me. Get the fuck off me. Get off me, you cunt. Who the fuck are you? Nobody fucks with me. Nobody.

THYESTES *has managed to pin him down.*

THYESTES: Calm down, brother. Go to sleep.
ATREUS: Hello, brother. What are you doing here?
THYESTES: Shh. Go to sleep.
ATREUS: He never could stand the sight of me, the old cunt. He always liked you better. I'm glad we're gone. It's just you and me now, brother. It's just you and me, isn't it?
THYESTES: Just you and me.
ATREUS: Everyone else can get fucked.
THYESTES: That's right. Just you and me.
ATREUS: I love you, mate.
THYESTES: I love you too.

ATREUS *eventually falls asleep.* THYESTES *checks on the kids inside the tent. He goes and sits next to* AEROPE. *He pours her a glass of wine.*

When we were born, I came out first. Everything was going well, I only took a few hours to arrive, I was breathing strong, healthy. Then he got stuck. He came testes first apparently. For a while there, my mum had a couple of balls sticking out of her vagina looking like some kind of she-man. The doctors were trying not to laugh. But it wasn't funny. The umbilical cord was getting compressed and not enough oxygen was reaching his brain and it took a couple of hours just to get his legs out and they were in a real hurry now because he could be getting brain damaged and his head was still stuck with one of his arms across his face and they had to twist him into all sorts of positions to get him out and when they did eventually get him free he was the most misshapen baby anyone had ever seen, from the forceps and the tugging. They had to put his little arm in a cast. He looked pretty funny. You should get him to show you the pictures Dad took. It took several days for them to find out whether or not he was retarded from the oxygen loss. But he was okay.

AEROPE *and* THYESTES *sit together in silence. He puts his arm around her.*

It's okay.

AEROPE *collapses into his shoulder and cries. She looks up at* THYESTES. *He leans in to kiss her.*

Curtain.

SCENE FIVE

SURTITLE: *'Atreus has found himself exiled again. He plots to take back the kingdom and reclaim his wife.'*

Curtain up. ATREUS *is on his own in the room. He has his phone plugged into some speakers and is listening to Aerope's voice on a voicemail message.*

AEROPE'S VOICE: Hi. honey, how's everything going?
ATREUS: Oh, you know, just hanging around.
AEROPE'S VOICE: I had my fingers crossed all day.
ATREUS: Oh, thanks, honey, I really appreciate that.
AEROPE'S VOICE: Listen, I was thinking I'd do a schnitzel tonight.
ATREUS: Schnitzel!
AEROPE'S VOICE: Does that sound good?
ATREUS: I love schnitzel!
AEROPE'S VOICE: Maybe with an onion sauce.
ATREUS: Oh, honey, you sure know how to tickle my insides.
AEROPE'S VOICE: I'm on my way to the supermarket, if you don't want the schnitzel call me and let me know.

ACT ONE 19

ATREUS: No, no, that's grand.
AEROPE'S VOICE: I'll probably be home at about seven.
ATREUS: Take your time. I've got some knitting I can do.
AEROPE'S VOICE: Oh, and don't forget to bring the Tupperware home.
ATREUS: Oh, the Tupperware. The Tupperware.
AEROPE'S VOICE: Love you so much. Bye, darling.
ATREUS: Oh, don't go, honey, I was having such a nice time chatting…
PHONE VOICE: 'To return the call press six. To transfer this message press fou—'

ATREUS has pressed a button on his phone.

Message received, third September at three fifty-nine p.m.
AEROPE'S VOICE: Hi honey, how's everything going?

The message plays again. He fits the following responses in.

ATREUS: Look, to be completely honest, it's a little tough right now. I found a lump under my armpit and I'm sure it's cancerous and I don't really think I'm ready to part this world yet so yeah I'm feeling a little on edge… Baby, do you think I'm going grey? I think I might be going grey. I can't find a mirror. Where'd you leave the mirror? Fuck the fucking Tupperware, where'd you leave the fucking mirror? Love you too. Sorry for shouting. Sorry.

He hangs up. He plays the message again. He can't think of what to say. He plays the message again.

I watched you sleeping one night. I had my gun in my hand and I was watching you sleeping. You looked so calm. You looked so bloody calm. And I wanted to cave your fucking face in with the butt of the pistol. But I said to myself, no, big guy, not a good idea, not a very good idea, grab a hold of yourself, she's your wife, she's not doing you any harm, look at her face, look at her poor innocent face. You were snoring just a little and it made me laugh. You see I had the chance. And I missed it.

He hangs up. He plays the message again.

Fuck you.
Fuck you.
Fuck you.
Fuck you.

FUCK YOU.
FUCK YOU.
FUCK YOU.
I HOPE YOU CHOKE ON HIS COCK.
Fuck you.

The phone starts making call-waiting noises. ATREUS *stops the voicemail replay and answers the phone, pulling it out of the speakers as he does so.*

Hello? Oh. Hi. Yeah. Well no, we need fifteen of them. If they can't do fifteen of them then we go elsewhere. We had a deal with them. I don't know where this is coming from. They absolutely have to be black. When have we ever hired a car from them that has not been black? This is really starting to get to me a little. I can feel myself getting angry. No I know that is not going to help anything. Okay. Well. How is that going to look if we show up with eight sedans and seven hatchbacks? Yeah. Not that great. Have they got a new manager or something? Is Joe still there? See if you can get him on the phone. This person sounds like a moron. Okay, okay. Listen, I want you to put it to them very simply and very clearly. Speak slow. Do You Want The Fucking Contract? Is the answer yes? Then Give Us What We Fucking Need. Tuesday. If I hear anything more about this I'm going to shit. Okay, ciao.

He hangs up and calls his voicemail. He replays the message and reconnects it to the speakers. He begins another conversation with the voicemail message.

Hey honey, you know what I really love about you? It's how supportive you are. Making the bed, ironing my shirts, cooking me schnitzels, fucking my brother, you turbo-slut. You really are the ticket. I have so much love for you. And this is how you repay me.

Curtain.

SCENE SIX

SURTITLE: *'Years of civil war, famine and disease have laid waste to Mycenae. Atreus has retaken control of the country. His forces capture Aerope and bring her to the palace.'*

ACT ONE

Curtain up. AEROPE *is giving* ATREUS *a blowjob. He's sitting in an armchair. The action is desperate and fast.* ATREUS *looks unaffected. Eventually he taps her on the back.*

ATREUS: Okay, sweetie. You can stop now. I'm sorry. I don't know what's got into me. I'm sorry. That was great. I guess I've just got a lot on my mind. Maybe we can try again later. Here, let me just get you sorted out.

He gets up and walks over to the other end of the room. He picks up a roll of gaffer tape.

I couldn't help but notice a bit of technique change there though, honey. Which disturbs me, you know. Why you're so good at that all of a sudden. Like someone's been giving you lessons. Come here, sweetie, let's get this on you.

He's pulled off a strip of tape. He puts in on her mouth.

There we go, sweetie. What time is it? I keep thinking it's seven, but maybe that's 'cause the clock's stopped. You look really good. Have you been getting back into yoga?

He puts on a pair of lacy women's underwear.

Hoo-wee. I am sweaty. I've been eating too much salt and not drinking enough water. I think not enough water makes me angry. Don't look at me. I'm hideous. I've put on a tonne. For a while I was eating butter by the spoonful. Just butter. You hungry? I'm starved. I'm like an empty bag in the stomach area. I was thinking I'd make you something special and I planned out all these recipes and things but I guess time got away from me. And I forgot. Ah, well. Let's not go crying over things that never happened. Doesn't matter. Let's put it behind us. What do you want for tucker? Hold on. I'll get some menus.

There are take-away menus scattered across the floor. He looks amongst them.

You like Thai? I'd go Thai. No Indian. I had, I must've had curry five times this week. Way too much curry. Should have seen it. Hoo-wee. I'll eat pizza, not Japanese, not Indian, Indian, Indian, Sri Lankan, Lebanese maybe. What's this one? Samoan. What do Samoans cook? Fucking mud crabs or something. Anyway, looks crap. Thai? Let's get Thai. I'll have those fishcakes and maybe a moneybag. You want a moneybag? I'm on my low-carb no-carb thing again. Put on a tonne. You pick. I'll have a salad. No meat. You want to sit down? You look tired. Come on. Let's sit down. You sit there. Oh, hey, I got the *Notebook* DVD. It's a special edition one with a whole lot of behind the scenes stuff. Oh, the present. Fuck. My mind is like a fucking sieve, Jesus. Need to get that looked at. What do you reckon? Early-onset dementia? Anyway listen to me, natter natter natter. I got you a present. Where'd I leave it? [*He clicks his fingers for a while, looking around.*] Sofa. [*He pulls up the seat of the armchair and pulls out a wrapped present.*] Open it. Go on, open it. See that paper? Organic. Nice, isn't it? There we go. [*The present is a dildo.*] Hello. [*He pulls it out of the box.*] Let's put this on you. [*He does.*] There you go. You like it? Feels good, right? That's good workmanship. Must be German or something. Jesus. You look so sexy.

He puts the dildo in his mouth. He sucks it for a while. He pushes her onto the armchair. He continues sucking the dildo.

Curtain.

END OF ACT ONE

ACT TWO

SCENE TWELVE

SURTITLE: *'Eighteen years later. Thyestes' prophecy is fulfilled. Atreus' adopted son, Aegisthus, has discovered his real father's identity. Aegisthus returns to Atreus with a message.'*

Curtain up. ATREUS *is sitting in an armchair, wearing a bathrobe and projecting slides against the wall. The slides are all pictures of two particular children and show them at various different times in their childhood.* AEGISTHUS *is standing in the corner of the room, with a gun in his hand.* ATREUS *continues watching slides as* AEGISTHUS *drums up the courage to kill him. Eventually* AEGISTHUS *raises his gun and shoots him.* ATREUS *sits dying as* AEGISTHUS *slides down the wall in shock.*

Curtain.

SCENE ELEVEN

SURTITLE: *'Pelopia, mother of Aegisthus and second wife of Atreus, has discovered the identity of Aegisthus' real father. Her discovery drives her to suicide.'*

PELOPIA *accompanies herself on a grand piano as she sings Schubert's 'Der Doppelgänger'.*

Curtain.

SCENE TEN

SURTITLE: *'Years after the death of Aerope, Atreus has chosen a new wife, Pelopia. He vows to raise her illegitimate son, Aegisthus, as his own.'*

Curtain up. ATREUS *is sitting against the wall, drinking from a champagne glass, a wine cooler with bottles in it next to him.* PELOPIA *stands watching him, a large present in her hand.*

PELOPIA: You okay?

ATREUS: Too much champagne.
PELOPIA: Champagne?
ATREUS: Yeah. I like calling it that. Sounds more bubbly.
PELOPIA: Really?
ATREUS: Yeah, you know how some things sound like the sound of their word?
PELOPIA: Yeah.
ATREUS: Like 'epiphany'.
PELOPIA: Yeah.
ATREUS: Sounds like what it is. You know the way those epiphanies just happen. Like, 'I just had an epiphany'.
PELOPIA: I get you.
ATREUS: Yeah.
PELOPIA: Did you really have an epiphany?
ATREUS: When?
PELOPIA: Just now.
ATREUS: I don't think so.
PELOPIA: Oh. That's disappointing.
ATREUS: No. Epiphanies are for the young.
PELOPIA: And you're an old man?
ATREUS: Dead right. No epiphanies for old men.
PELOPIA: Sad.
ATREUS: No. Better.
PELOPIA: How?
ATREUS: No more surprises. Everything's nice and even.
PELOPIA: Nice and even?
ATREUS: Calm. Makes sense. Beautiful girl. Kiss me. Sweetie, there seems to be an object in the way of our affections.
PELOPIA: Bought us presents.
ATREUS: Is that what that was, I was wondering what that was.
PELOPIA: Yeah.
ATREUS: What is it?
PELOPIA: Open it up.
ATREUS: Feels soft.
PELOPIA: Yeah.
ATREUS: Doesn't rattle.
PELOPIA: Just open it.

ACT TWO

ATREUS: I like to guess.
PELOPIA: Don't think you will.
ATREUS: Isn't ticking. That's a good sign.
PELOPIA: Come on.
ATREUS: I give up.
PELOPIA: Open it.

> ATREUS *opens the gift and takes out two bathrobes.*

ATREUS: Oh no, you didn't. His and hers.
PELOPIA: Yeah.
ATREUS: You're a cack.
PELOPIA: For an old man.
ATREUS: Too funny.
PELOPIA: And his old woman.

> *They kiss.*

ATREUS: You're not so old.
PELOPIA: I'm cold.
ATREUS: You're cold and I'm old.
PELOPIA: Ha ha.
ATREUS: Why don't you put your dressing-gown on?
PELOPIA: You too.

> *They put on their bathrobes. One has 'R' embroidered on it and the other 'C'.*

ATREUS: Sweetie, I do have one quick question though. Who is 'R' and who is 'C'? Whose dressing-gowns are these? Who did you kill to get these?
PELOPIA: [*laughing*] I didn't kill anyone. I got them embroidered. 'R' for Roy.
ATREUS: Roy?
PELOPIA: Roy Orbison.
ATREUS: You got me a Roy Orbison dressing-gown?
PELOPIA: It's not actually—
ATREUS: Don't speak.

> *He kisses her.*

Who's 'C', baby?
PELOPIA: It's Claudette. His wife.

ATREUS: That's an interesting choice. A lot of people would have gone, his second wife.
PELOPIA: I didn't know he had a second wife.
ATREUS: He did. And that lasted a little longer. Unfortunately the lovely Claudette was killed in a car crash two years into their marriage.
PELOPIA: Maybe I can get it changed to his second wife.
ATREUS: No, I wouldn't. I think Claudette was always his real love. The first cut is the deepest. You know that two years after Claudette passed away, he lost their two kids in a house fire? Can you believe that?
PELOPIA: I'm really beginning to regret this decision.
ATREUS: That's where the voice came from. He understood the pain. Thank you so much, sweetie.
PELOPIA: I'm glad you like it.
ATREUS: Give me a kiss.

They kiss.

PELOPIA: You taste of cigarettes.
ATREUS: I was smoking.
PELOPIA: Thought you stopped.
ATREUS: Just tonight.
PELOPIA: And champagnee.
ATREUS: 'Champagnee'. James Cagney.
PELOPIA: Who's James Cagney?
ATREUS: Thirties gangster movie star.
PELOPIA: How do you know this stuff?
ATREUS: TCM. Turner Classic Movies.
PELOPIA: Give me some of that champagnee, James Cagney.

She drinks.

ATREUS: You alright?
PELOPIA: Yeah.
ATREUS: Good.
PELOPIA: I love that word. 'Alright'.
ATREUS: Yeah?
PELOPIA: Yeah. You can say it so many different ways.
ATREUS: How'd you mean?
PELOPIA: Like something can be crap you can say, 'oh… it was alright' or something can be great and you can say, 'it's alright!'

ATREUS: What am I?
PELOPIA: You're alright.
ATREUS: You said it different that time.
PELOPIA: Yeah.
ATREUS: What kind of alright was that?
PELOPIA: That was good alright.
ATREUS: Yeah?
PELOPIA: Yeah. The best.
ATREUS: Alright!
PELOPIA: You're funny.
ATREUS: Am I?
PELOPIA: You know you are.
ATREUS: I don't know that.
PELOPIA: Yeah, you do. You make me laugh all the time.
ATREUS: I can't remember doing that.
PELOPIA: Yes you can.
ATREUS: Can't remember what your laugh sounds like.
PELOPIA: Yeah, you can.
ATREUS: No I can't.
PELOPIA: You're just a little trashed.
ATREUS: Yeah. I am. Feel good though.
PELOPIA: Yeah?
ATREUS: Yeah.
PELOPIA: Good.
ATREUS: Can we go home now please?
PELOPIA: Isn't time yet.
ATREUS: Tonight's our time we can go when we please.
PELOPIA: Just a little longer.
ATREUS: Anything you want.

They sing Roy Orbison's 'Anything You Want' together.

Curtain.

SCENE NINE

SURTITLE: 'Thyestes rapes his own daughter, Pelopia. Pelopia remains ignorant of her rapist's identity.'

Curtain up. THYESTES *has just raped his daughter,* PELOPIA. *She is in the foetal position, crying. He is shocked at his own act, stumbling around half-naked.*

Curtain.

SCENE EIGHT

SURTITLE: *'Thyestes has been driven mad by Atreus' horrific act. He receives a prophecy that a child by his own daughter, Pelopia, will one day kill Atreus and avenge him.'*

Curtain up. THYESTES *is sitting in a wheelchair, clothed only in a nappy, watching a BBC wildlife documentary. He has an intravenous drip attached to his arm. This continues for a long while in silence. Eventually, the sound of children's voices in a choral arrangement.*

Curtain.

SCENE SEVEN

SURTITLE: *'Several years have passed since Atreus reclaimed the throne of Mycenae. The country has returned to a period of relative calm. Thyestes has settled with his family in a distant land. A message from Atreus arrives, inviting Thyestes to return home and share the throne again. After much deliberation, Thyestes accepts the offer. He arrives in Mycenae with his family. That night, a reconciliation feast is prepared by Atreus. Unbeknown to Thyestes, Atreus has killed Thyestes' children, dismembered and cooked them for the feast.'*

Curtain up. THYESTES *and* ATREUS *are eating dinner.* ATREUS *is serving meat sauce onto spaghetti. He hands a plate to* THYESTES, *then serves himself and sits down to eat.*

THYESTES: I used some old wood that I found on a farm.
ATREUS: Right.
THYESTES: Sanded it back, made a table.
ATREUS: A table?
THYESTES: A dining table.
ATREUS: Yeah, right.
THYESTES: Each piece of wood has a life of its own.

ACT TWO

ATREUS: What do you mean?
THYESTES: Different lines, different histories—depending on where the wood came from.
ATREUS: Okay.
THYESTES: How old it was when it was cut down.
ATREUS: Yeah, right.
THYESTES: What kind of weather it was exposed to over its life.
ATREUS: Yeah, that makes sense.
THYESTES: You can see it in the lines of the wood.
ATREUS: Right.
THYESTES: See what kind of life it's had.
ATREUS: Wow.
THYESTES: You make a table, bring a whole bunch of these bits of wood together and you've got all these different lives resting next to each other.
ATREUS: Like a graveyard.
THYESTES: Hm?
ATREUS: Like a cemetery for bits of wood.
THYESTES: Except it's a table.
ATREUS: Bit morbid.
THYESTES: What?
ATREUS: Thinking about death every time you sit down to eat.
THYESTES: It's just a table.
ATREUS: I know.
THYESTES: They're just bits of wood, you don't have to think too much about it.
ATREUS: I think I would. I think I'd be thinking about death.
THYESTES: Right.
ATREUS: Hey, remember that tree we used to climb when we were kids?
THYESTES: We climbed lots of trees.
ATREUS: The dead one.
THYESTES: Oh yeah, in that park.
ATREUS: Yeah.
THYESTES: Got struck by lightning.
ATREUS: Huge tree.
THYESTES: Massive.
ATREUS: Wonder if it's still there?

THYESTES: Wonder if it's as big as we remember?
ATREUS: Yeah.
THYESTES: Probably tiny.
ATREUS: Yeah that's funny, isn't it?
THYESTES: I drove past our old house the other day.
ATREUS: Oh, yeah?
THYESTES: Yeah. Drove up the killer hill.
ATREUS: The killer hill, what was that again?
THYESTES: That hill we called the killer hill because there was no way you could ride your bike up it.
ATREUS: That's right. I forgot about that hill. There was always a rumour that some guy had ridden down it and fallen off and knocked all his teeth out.
THYESTES: Probably wasn't even true.
ATREUS: Probably something our parents made up so we wouldn't ride down it.
THYESTES: Like that whole thing how there was a paedophile or a rapist at the back of the oval at school.
ATREUS: Funny how people do that.
THYESTES: What?
ATREUS: Make up scary shit to scare their kids out of doing things.
THYESTES: Yeah.
ATREUS: I guess those kinds of people are out there though.
THYESTES: Huh?
ATREUS: Paedophiles and rapists and what not.
THYESTES: Yeah.
ATREUS: Can't trust everyone.
THYESTES: Anyway the killer hill isn't so killer.
ATREUS: What?
THYESTES: The hill. It's not so steep.
ATREUS: Oh yeah?
THYESTES: Not so killer.
ATREUS: Right.
THYESTES: Probably like the tree.
ATREUS: Yeah.
THYESTES: That's probably not as big as we remember.
ATREUS: What'd we call it again? We had a name for it.

ACT TWO

THYESTES: Did we?
ATREUS: Yeah.
THYESTES: It was from one of those Berenstain Bear books.
ATREUS: I'd forgot about the Berenstain Bears.
THYESTES: They lived in a tree, the whole family, but it was dark and scary…
ATREUS: The spooky old tree.
THYESTES: That's right.
ATREUS: The spooky old tree. That's what we called that tree in the park.
THYESTES: I used to have nightmares about that tree.
ATREUS: Nightmares?
THYESTES: It was weird. I don't really remember it but it's still the scariest dream I've ever had.
ATREUS: Uh-huh.
THYESTES: I remember being trapped in the tree. There'd been this barbeque and the weather changed and everything was being packed up and everybody was leaving. I could hear Mum and Dad calling me but I couldn't get out of the tree.
ATREUS: Whoa.
THYESTES: When I woke up I was sweating and in a panic and that's what I kept saying to Mum and Dad.
ATREUS: What?
THYESTES: Hm?
ATREUS: What were you saying?
THYESTES: I can't get out of the tree. I can't get out of the tree.
ATREUS: What did Mum and Dad say?
THYESTES: They didn't know what the fuck I was talking about. Funny.
ATREUS: What's funny?
THYESTES: I don't know. They're the clearest memories I have.
ATREUS: Which ones?
THYESTES: From when we were kids.
ATREUS: Oh yeah?
THYESTES: The colour of my board shorts at the beach.
ATREUS: Oh yeah?
THYESTES: The nut mix in the car Mum and Dad would eat.
ATREUS: Oh yeah?
THYESTES: Brazil nuts. Hated the brazil nut.

ATREUS: Really?
THYESTES: Yeah. Didn't know the name for it then though. Just knew I didn't like the big ones.
ATREUS: I like brazil nuts. You should have told me. We could have swapped.
THYESTES: I like them now. I wonder why that is?
ATREUS: Your taste matures I guess.
THYESTES: No, I wonder why I remember all of that old stuff so well, but last week or last month is just a blur.
ATREUS: Just age.
THYESTES: I guess.
ATREUS: The memory fades.
THYESTES: Yeah.
ATREUS: Whoa.
THYESTES: What?
ATREUS: Nothing. [*Pause. Referring to a photo album that has been lying on the table*] What are they doing here?
THYESTES: Give me a look.
ATREUS: This one here. They look like nuns.
THYESTES: Oh. I think they were judges that day.
ATREUS: Judges?
THYESTES: Yeah, they were high court judges.
ATREUS: Oh yeah? What was the case?
THYESTES: I think I'd stolen a lollipop.
ATREUS: That's not so bad.
THYESTES: They gave me life.
ATREUS: That's harsh.
THYESTES: Yeah.
ATREUS: Least you didn't get the chop.
THYESTES: There's that.
ATREUS: This one's cute.
THYESTES: Which one's that?
ATREUS: This one with the tutu.
THYESTES: Oh yeah. They were dancing.
ATREUS: Cute.

   Pause.

ACT TWO

THYESTES: What about you?
ATREUS: What about me?
THYESTES: Nightmares.
ATREUS: What?
THYESTES: What's your worst nightmare?
ATREUS: Never had one.
THYESTES: What are you talking about you've never had one?
ATREUS: Just never had one.
THYESTES: Everyone has them.
ATREUS: Not me.
THYESTES: You probably just don't remember.
ATREUS: I don't think so.
THYESTES: Must be something to do with your sleep patterns.
ATREUS: What?
THYESTES: You have to wake up in the right stage. Otherwise you don't remember them.
ATREUS: I sleep like a baby.
THYESTES: That's it.
ATREUS: Except when I don't sleep.
THYESTES: Right.
ATREUS: And then I don't sleep at all.
THYESTES: Uh-huh.
ATREUS: Oh, hang on.
THYESTES: What?
ATREUS: There was this one time.
THYESTES: Oh yeah?
ATREUS: When we went to Malaysia. I woke up and I thought I was still at home. And I pissed on Mum and Dad's bed.
THYESTES: Oh yeah. That was funny.
ATREUS: Because at home that was where the toilet was.

> THYESTES *laughs*.

That's a nightmare, right?
THYESTES: Not really.
ATREUS: No?
THYESTES: You were just disoriented.
ATREUS: Oh.

Silence. Eating.

Remember.
THYESTES: Remember what?
ATREUS: Oh. I was just saying it.
THYESTES: Okay.
ATREUS: It's just one of those words.
THYESTES: Yeah.
ATREUS: Sounds like what it is.
THYESTES: Huh?
ATREUS: Remember. Remember. Remember. Remember. Remember. Remember. Remember. Remember. Remember. Remember. Remember.

Curtain.

The following section is the equivalent of a montage sequence in cinema. The curtain goes up and down quickly, revealing a series of moments that follow Thyestes' discovery of having eaten his own children. The curtain acts as a fast-forward device.

Curtain up. THYESTES *has discovered he has eaten his own children. He is vomiting into his plate.* ATREUS *is laughing.*

Curtain.

Curtain up. THYESTES *is still vomiting, against the wall.* ATREUS *is performing a victory dance.*

Curtain.

Curtain up. AEROPE *has arrived home and is screaming at* ATREUS. THYESTES *is huddled in the corner.*

Curtain.

Curtain up. AEROPE *is bleeding from a gunshot to her head and staggering around the room.* ATREUS *shoots her dead and she falls to the ground.* THYESTES *discovers her corpse beside him and reels back in horror.*

Curtain.

Curtain up. ATREUS *is dancing with the wall and waving his gun around.*

Curtain.

ACT TWO 35

Curtain up. THYESTES *is holding* ATREUS' *gun against his head and begging to be put out of his misery.* ATREUS *is shouting in victory.*

Tastes good, huh? Tastes good. This is how it feels. You like that? They were calling for you. They were calling out your name. Calling, 'Dad!' 'Dad!' 'Dad!'

Blackout.

THE END

Belvoir and Sydney Festival, in association with Carriageworks, present

THYESTES

By **THOMAS HENNING, CHRIS RYAN, SIMON STONE
& MARK WINTER** after **SENECA**
Director **SIMON STONE**
Originally created by **THE HAYLOFT PROJECT**

This production of Thyestes *opened at Carriageworks on
Wednesday 18 January 2012.*

Set & Costume Designer **CLAUDE MARCOS**
Lighting Designer **GOVIN RUBEN**
Composer & Sound Designer **STEFAN GREGORY**
Dramaturg **ANNE-LOUISE SARKS**
Technical Manager **NEIL FISHER**
Head Mechanist **WARREN SUTTON**
Stage Manager **EVA TANDY**
Assistant Stage Manager **REBECCA POULTER**

Performed by
**THOMAS HENNING
CHRIS RYAN
MARK WINTER**

Thyestes premiered in September 2010, in the Tower Theatre, Malthouse, as a Malthouse Theatre commission – a result of Malthouse Theatre's In Residence Program, made possible with support from The Sidney Myer Fund. The premiere production was supported by the Victorian Government through Arts Victoria and through Interconnections, an initiative of the Australia Council, the Australian Government's arts funding and advisory body.

THANK YOU

THE HAYLOFT PROJECT 2011: Benedict Hardie, Claude Marcos, Martina Murray, Carl Nilsson-Polias, Anne-Louise Sarks.
Also: Stephen Armstrong, Michael Kantor, Malthouse Theatre, Jo Porter, Lucy Birkinshaw, Caitlin Byrne, Ann Tonks.

Images Jeff Busby. Malthouse Theatre 2010 season. Reproduced with kind permission.
Design Alphabet Studio

Chris & Mark

Co-Writer & Director Note

Simon Stone

In May of 2010, Mark Winter, Thomas Henning and I spent a few weeks drinking mineral water and eating grapefruits in an office overlooking Johnston Street, Fitzroy. We were trying to come up with a framework for our new version of the Ancient Greek myth of Thyestes and his brother Atreus. We'd read a very academic translation of Seneca's Roman play of the myth back in April with Chris Ryan (who was now in Sydney doing *Measure for Measure* at Belvoir) and we'd settled on the notion of expanding the limited timescale of the Seneca play to encompass the larger chain of retributive killings in the original myth.

In between trips to Coles to buy supplies, we read up on our mythology, poured over Wiki articles on various tyrants, dictators, serial killers and psychopaths, scribbled on the wall the beginnings of a plot structure, scribbled over it and started again, until we had the spine of what is presented in this play. We were fascinated by the psychology, of both perpetrator and victim, underlying the horrific acts in the myth. We weren't content to accept the characters or the events in the story as fabulous inventions of the past. We wanted to explore the aspects of Greek mythology that drove Freud to use these stories as clues to our own more modern but no less brutal instincts. Eventually we realised that the way into this psychological terrain would be to present a series of moments between atrocities, a selection of conversations amidst the terror, and to play these scenes in as modern and realistic a way as possible.

We went through and selected all the most significant moments in the life-long rivalry between Atreus and Thyestes, from the first killing to the last. For the first half of the play we wrote scenes leading up to those moments and for the second half we wrote scenes in the aftermath of them. Essentially, a plot structure exploring in one half cause and in the other effect (both of which of course inevitably become the other).

At the centre of this movement from cause to effect, as the lynchpin of the production, we put the famous dinner scene that provides the larger part of Seneca's play. In order to retain this scene as the climax of the story, we reversed the order of second half of the play, so that both halves of the play head inexorably towards this horrific night, one forwards in time and one backwards. By the time you watch the concluding scene, you have witnessed both the motivations and repercussions leading to and resulting from the event taking place onstage.

With this synopsis in place we parted ways and returned in late July for beginning of rehearsals at the Malthouse Theatre. Now with Chris in the writing team, we covered the walls of the theatre with more and more detailed versions of the plot. Eventually we were ready to write and we divided the scenes between each other, wrote a draft, then handed it on for redrafting by one of the others. We rehearsed the scenes as we wrote them, improvised on their basic structure, documented this new text, rewrote the scenes, re-rehearsed them, improvised again, rewrote and so on into previews and throughout the season. Often we would discard a whole scene, begin from a new improvisation, approach from a different angle or replace dialogue with action or music until we felt that the whole production was rhythmically and tonally in tune with the source material.

Through this process we were able to bring a naturalness to the language that was in stark contrast to the heightened nature of the myth. The tension between the horror of the plot and the almost callous minimalism of the performances was born of a desire to reassert these myths' essential humanity. To say, these people do exist. They live in our world. They've always been here and they always will be. They're not monsters or half-animals or gods. They're humans, and that's what makes them so terrifying.

Synopsis

Ancient Greece, The Kingdom of Pisa. King Pelops has declared his bastard child Chrysippus heir to the throne. His queen Hippodamia convinces Pelops' rightful heirs, her sons Atreus and Thyestes, to kill their half-brother.

Upon discovering the murder of Chrysippus, Pelops exiles Atreus and Thyestes along with their mother. Unable to bear the separation from her husband and the humiliation of exile, Hippodamia kills herself.

Through various political manoeuvrings, Atreus and Thyestes have found themselves joint kings of Mycenae. Atreus chooses a wife, Aerope. An agreement is made between the brothers to take it in turns to rule, and that whoever is on the throne takes possession of a golden ram.

After years of calm rule, Thyestes steals the golden ram and seduces Atreus' wife Aerope.

Thyestes taunts Atreus that he will only return the kingdom when the sun moves backwards through the sky. Atreus enlists the help of the god Hermes and achieves this miraculous feat.

Although back in power, Atreus is unable to put thoughts of revenge out of his mind. He plots to kill his brother's children and feed them to him. This atrocity is dedicated to his grandfather, Tantulus, who fed his son Pelops to the Olympian gods in a test of their omniscience.

Atreus' plan succeeds. Invited back for a reconciliatory feast, Thyestes unwittingly eats his own children.

Driven mad by this horrific act, Thyestes consults an oracle, and is told that a child by his own daughter Pelopia will one day kill Atreus.

Discovering her at a feast in the forest one night, Thyestes rapes Pelopia, who is unaware of the identity of her assailant. She does, however, manage to steal his sword.

Pelopia travels to Mycenae and comes to the attention of Atreus, who, ignorant of her identity decides to marry her. He takes in her illegitimate son and the product of her rape, Aegisthus, and vows to raise him as his own son.

Despite the marriage, Pelopia is unable to recover from the trauma of her rape and kills herself.

When Aegisthus reaches adulthood, Atreus gives him the sword that Pelopia stole from her rapist and encourages Aegisthus to find him and kill him.

Following the trail of the sword, Aegisthus discovers Thyestes, who reveals the horrors committed by Atreus at the feast. He returns to Atreus and avenges his true father, Thyestes.

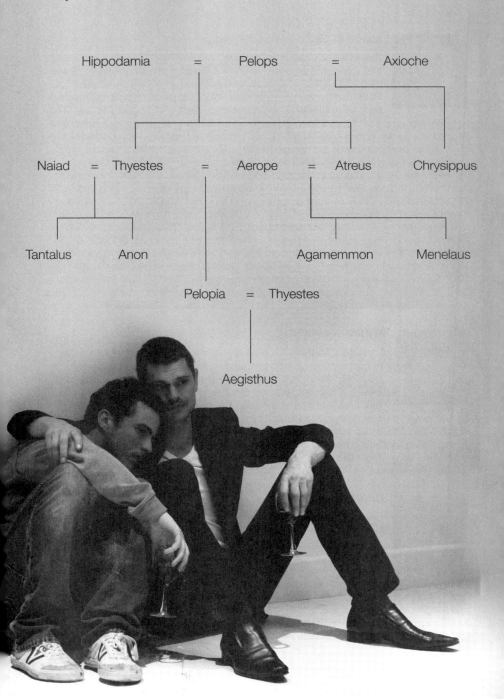

Biographies

SIMON STONE Co-Writer and Director

Simon is a graduate of the Victorian College of the Arts. In 2007 he founded the independent ensemble The Hayloft Project. For Hayloft he co-wrote and directed *Thyestes*, which was commissioned by and originally produced at Malthouse Theatre (winner of 2010 Green Room Awards for Best Production, Best Adaptation and Best Ensemble), co-wrote and directed *The Only Child* (with B Sharp, winner of Sydney Theatre Award for Best Independent Production), adapted and directed *The Suicide*, *Spring Awakening* (both with B Sharp) and *Platonov*, was one third of the multi-director project *3xSisters*, and directed Rita Kalnejais' *B.C*. In 2009 Simon directed *The Promise* for Belvoir and in 2011 he became the company's Resident Director. In his first year in the role, Simon wrote and directed *The Wild Duck* after Ibsen (winner of three 2011 Helpmann Awards, including Best Play; five 2011 Sydney Theatre Award nominations, including Best Production and Best Direction) and directed *Neighbourhood Watch* (four 2011 Sydney Theatre Award nominations, including Best Production). For Sydney Theatre Company and Malthouse Melbourne, Simon co-translated and directed *Baal* (2011 Sydney Theatre Award nomination for Best Direction). As an actor, Simon performed in Belvoir's 2007 production of *Who's Afraid of Virginia Woolf?* and appeared in the films *Jindabyne*, *Kokoda*, *Balibo*, *Blame* and *Eye of the Storm*. Simon was the 2008 recipient of the biennial George Fairfax Memorial Award. Later in 2012, Simon will be writing and directing *Strange Interlude* (after Eugene O'Neill) and directing *Death of a Salesman* for Belvoir, as well as a stage version of Ingmar Bergman's film *Face to Face* for Sydney Theatre Company.

THOMAS HENNING Co-Writer and Performer

For Belvoir, **Thomas** has previously appeared in *The Business*. In 2009 he co-wrote *The Only Child* which was a B Sharp/The Hayloft Project production. He is the co-creator and director of Black Lung Theatre, where his writing and directing credits include *Rubeville and Glasoon* and *Avast*. Thomas has worked as writer/actor with Melbourne's The Hayloft Project on *3xSisters*, *The Only Child* and most recently *Thyestes*. *Rubeville* won a series of awards including Best Production at the Melbourne and Adelaide Fringe Festivals, The Adelaide Touring Award and Best of the Fest at the Adelaide Fringe. Thomas received Best Adaptation at the 2010 Green Room Awards for his work on *Thyestes*, which also received Best Ensemble and Best Production.

CHRIS RYAN Co-Writer and Performer

Chris was co-writer on Simon Stone's version of *The Wild Duck*, for Belvoir's 2011 Season. As an actor Chris' theatre credits include *Measure for Measure* and *The Promise* for Belvoir; *Gross und Klein* (Sydney Theatre Company); *Baal*, *Tis Pity She's a Whore* and *Elizabeth* (Malthouse Theatre); *Concussion* (Sydney Theatre Company/Griffin Theatre Company); *The Hypocrite* (Melbourne Theatre Company); *The Call* (Griffin Theatre Company); *Hamlet*, *Othello* (Bell Shakespeare); *Thyestes* and *Platonov* (The Hayloft Project). Chris also featured in the short film *Numurkah*, which screened at FedFest 2009. Chris received a Sydney Theatre Award nomination for Best Newcomer for his role in *Othello* and a Green Room Award nomination for Best Male Performance for *Platonov*. *The Wild Duck* won Best Play at the 2011 Helpmann Awards.

MARK WINTER Co-Writer and Performer

Mark completed the acting program at the Victorian College of the Arts in 2005, under Lindy Davies. Mark works as an actor, writer and director with Black Lung Theatre and The Hayloft Project. Both companies are nationally recognised as harbingers of innovative and thought-provoking productions and both have earned a slew of awards. His feature film credits include *Balibo*, *Van Diemen's Land*, *Blame*, *Playing for Charlie* and *Triple Happiness*. Mark also appeared in HBO Television's *The Pacific*, produced by Steven Spielberg and Tom Hanks. Other TV credits include *Winners and Losers*, *Killing Time* and *Rush*. Mark also plays internet sensation Detective Larry Hard in *Cop Hard*, a webisode series. *Thyestes* was awarded Best Production, Best Ensemble and Best Adaptation at the 2010 Green Room Awards. Mark was also recognised for his performance as Atreus with a Best Actor nomination.

NEIL FISHER Technical Manager

Neil is a graduate of NIDA's technical production course. Most recently he was production consultant on the Belvoir/Urban Theatre Projects/Sydney Festival production of *Buried City*. Neil worked as technical manager on the national tour of *Namatjira* (Belvoir/Big hART) and *Ngapartji Ngapartji* for the Sydney (Belvoir/Big hART/Sydney Festival), Ernabella and Alice Springs seasons. As a freelance technician he has worked for Bangarra Dance Theatre in various positions including technical manager, lighting designer and head electrician on their productions of *Fire*, *Mathinna*, *Awakenings*, *True Stories*, *Clan* and *Spirit*. Prior to Bangarra, Neil worked for Ensemble Productions as their production manager on *Six Dance Lessons in Six Weeks*, *End of the Rainbow*, *Are You There*, *Local Man* and *Drawer Boy*. As the resident head electrician for Pinchgut Opera, Neil has worked on *The Fairy Queen*, *L'Orfeo*, *Dardanus*, *Idomeneo*, *Juditha Triumphans*, *David & Jonathan*, *L'Ormindo*, *Orpheus & Eurydice* and, most recently, *Griselda*.

Chris, Mark & Thomas

Mark & Thomas

Chris

STEFAN GREGORY Composer & Sound Designer

Stefan was an associate artist at Belvoir in 2011, and has been composer and sound designer of Belvoir's productions of *As You Like It, Neighbourhood Watch* (in which he also played the chemist), *The Seagull, The Wild Duck, Measure for Measure* and *That Face,* and performed as a guitarist in *Peribanez.* He also composed and performed in *The War of the Roses* and *Frankenstein* (Sydney Theatre Company). Other theatre credits include *A Midsummer Night's Dream* (B Sharp/Bob Presents/Arts Radar); *Ladybird* (B Sharp/Small Things Productions); *Baal* (Malthouse Theatre/Sydney Theatre Company); *Thyestes, The Suicide, B.C.* (The Hayloft Project); *Silent Disco, The Call* (Griffin Theatre Company); *King Lear, Hamlet* and *Othello* (Bell Shakespeare Company). Stefan has been nominated for Sydney Theatre Awards for Best Score or Sound Design for *Baal* and *Measure for Measure*, and a Helpmann Award for *Baal*. His work with the band Faker has earned him a Jack Award, a platinum single and several ARIA nominations.

CLAUDE MARCOS Set & Costume Designer

Since graduating from the West Australian Academy of Performing Arts in 2005, **Claude** has designed a number of productions including *The Trial* (Malthouse/Sydney Theatre Company/ThinIce); *The Dead Man's Cell Phone, Return to Earth* (Melbourne Theatre Company); *3xSisters, The Only Child, B.C, The Suicide, Delectable Shelter* (The Hayloft Project); *Thyestes* (Malthouse/The Hayloft Project); *The Duel* (Sydney Theatre Company/ThinIce); *Thom Pain (based on nothing)* (Arts Radar/B Sharp); *Rhinoceros* (Union House Theatre); *Woyzeck* and *Honour* (Black Swan State Theatre Company); *The Goat or who is Sylvia?, Loveplay, Glorious! Speed the Plow* and *Tender Napalm* (Perth Theatre Company); *The Goose Chase* and *Red Shoes* (ThinIce). He also worked as the exhibition designer for *Suzie Wong, Hong Kong* (Vincent Fantauzzo), *The Creek 1977* (Vincent Fantauzzo, Baz Luhrmann), and *Million Puppets Projects* UNIMA Festival 2007. Claude is currently working on commissions for Perth Theatre Company and is an associate artist with The Hayloft Project.

REBECCA POULTER Assistant Stage Manager

Rebecca is a graduate of NIDA's production course and Swinburne University of Technology. She was stage manager for *Actor on a Box* (Sydney Theatre Company); *Judith* (The Impending Room/Tamarama Rock Surfers); *The Secret of the Seven Marbles* (Tamarama Rock Surfers); *John and Jen* (Sidetrack Theatre); *Women of Troy* (Cell Block Theatre); *Mash Up* (Q Theatre Company); *Romeo and Juliet* (Eagle's Nest); *Orestes 2.0* (Griffin Theatre Company); *The Comedy of Errors* (Shakespeare on the Green). As assistant stage manager her credits include *Blood Wedding, ZEBRA!, True West* and *The Comedy of Errors* (Sydney Theatre Company). As production stage manager Rebecca worked on *The Ugly One, Shining City* (Griffin Theatre Company); *Pictures of Bright Lights* (Little Ones Theatre Company/Tamarama Rock Surfers). She was technical stage manager for the Melbourne International Comedy Festival, and lighting and sound operator for *Arj Barker*. Rebecca has also held roles with Sydney Festival, Sydney Fringe Festival and Blue Fish Events.

GOVIN RUBEN Lighting Designer

Govin holds a Bachelor of Dramatic Arts (Production) majoring in Lighting Design from the Victorian College of the Arts. Previously for Belvoir, he has designed *And They Called Him Mr Glamour*. Govin also designed *20 Years of The Pants* (The Pants/Adelaide Fringe Festival) and *Hatch* (Ishara Puppet Festival, New Delhi). Previous designs for The Black Lung include *Kissy Kissy* (Adelaide Fringe Festival), *Avast* and *Avast II: The Welshman Cometh*. In 2012 he will make his Sydney Dance Company debut with *Vs Macbeth*. Govin's awards include the Orloff Family Trusts Scholarship for outstanding achievement while at VCA, and Green Room nominations for Best Lighting Design for *Kissy Kissy* and *Avast II*. Govin would like to thank Luke Hails and Kay Wengierek for inspiring him in the field of lighting design.

ANNE-LOUISE SARKS Dramaturg

Anne-Louise has a BA Honours in Performance Studies from The University of Sydney and a BDA from the Victorian College of the Arts. In 2011, she was director in residence at the Malthouse and a Belvoir associate artist. While at Belvoir she worked as assistant director on *The Wild Duck*. Anne-Louise is Artistic Director of The Hayloft Project. In 2012 she will direct *The Seed* at Melbourne Theatre Company and a new production of *Medea* at Belvoir. For The Hayloft Project, Anne-Louise co-wrote and directed *The Nest* (after Gorky), and was director and dramaturg on *Yuri Wells*. As an actor her credits include *Return to Earth* (Melbourne Theatre Company), *3 X Sisters* (The Hayloft Project), *The Only Child* and *The Suicide* (B Sharp/The Hayloft Project), *The Spook* (Malthouse Theatre), *YES* and *Five Kinds of Silence* (OpticNerve Performance Group).

EVA TANDY Stage Manager

This is **Eva**'s debut production with Belvoir. Her credits as stage manager include *The Joy of Text, Life Without Me, Dead Man's Cell Phone, The Ugly One* (Melbourne Theatre Company); *Porn.Cake, Avast, Avast II: The Welshman Cometh* (The Black Lung); *Song of the Bleeding Throat* (11th Hour Theatre); *Shadow Boxing* (The Groundswell Division); *Platonov: Recut* (The Hayloft Project). As assistant stage manager her credits include *Clybourne Park, Madagascar, God of Carnage, The Man from Mukinupin, Realism, Cat on a Hot Tin Roof, The 39 Steps, The Season at Sarsaparilla, Don's Party, Enlightenment, Festen, The Give and Take* and *A Single Act* (Melbourne Theatre Company). Eva is also a founding member of, and producer for, The Groundswell Division.

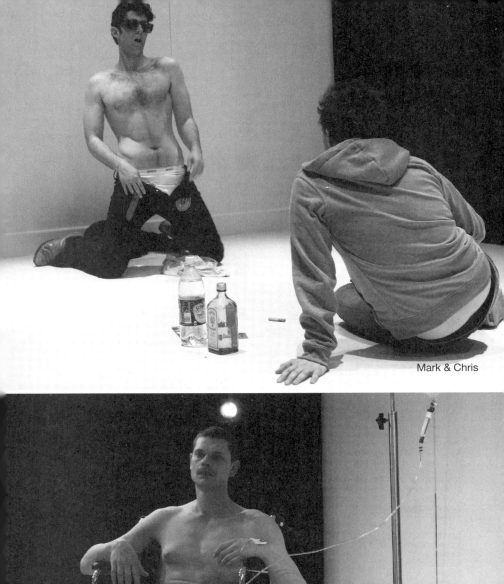

Mark & Chris

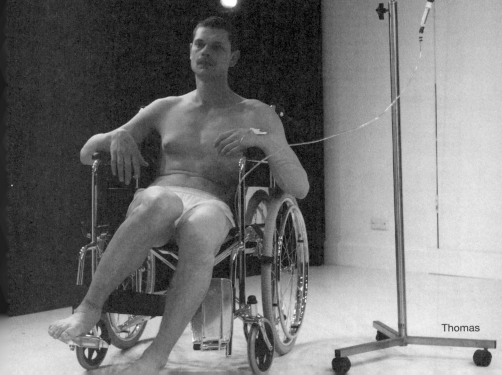

Thomas

sydney festival 2012

Sydney Festival Limited
Level 2, 10 Hickson Road
The Rocks NSW 2000
Tel: 61 2 8248 6500
sydneyfestival.org.au

PATRON
Her Excellency
Professor Marie Bashir AC CVO
Governor of New South Wales

BOARD OF DIRECTORS
President
The Hon. Barry O'Farrell MP
Premier of New South Wales
Chair
Clover Moore MP
Lord Mayor of Sydney
Directors
The Hon. George Souris MP
Monica Barone
Simon Corah
Matthew Melhuish
Sam Weiss
Geoff Wilson
Alternate Directors
Barry Buffier
(for The Hon. Barry O'Farrell MP)
Clr Phillip Black
(for The Lord Mayor of Sydney)
Mary Darwell
(for The Hon. George Souris MP)
Ann Hoban (for Monica Barone)

SYDNEY FESTIVAL STAFF
Festival Director
Lindy Hume
Executive Director
Josephine Ridge

ADMINISTRATION
Financial Controller
Tanya Bush
Accountant
Francesca Hendricks
Payroll
Carina Mision
Executive Assistant
Rachael McNally
Executive Office Projects Coordinator
Fiona Jackson
Administration Officer
Julie Gock
Receptionists
Rebecca Hunter
Taline Vesmadian

PROGRAMMING
Head of Programming
Bill Harris
Program Manager
Danni Colgan
Programming Associate
Adam McGowan
Special Projects
Loretta Busby
Travel & Artist Coordinator
Edwina Perrotta
Project Manager
Hannah Sanders
Music Coordinator
Janna Hayes
Program Administrator
Ella McNeill
Project Coordinator
Erica McCalman

MARKETING
Head of Marketing, Communications & Digital Strategy
Jill Colvin
Marketing Manager
Derek Gilchrist
Marketing Coordinator
Linly Goh
Digital Marketing Coordinator
Julia Thomas
Publicity Manager
Sarah Wilson
Publicists
Jane Davis
Charlotte Greig
Design Manager
Mary Simpson
Signage Coordinator
Franzisca Geis
Volunteer Program Coordinator
Josh Wheatley

TICKETING
Ticketing & Planning Manager
Simon Keen
Ticketing Coordinator
Sarah Neville
Ticketing Guest Services Coordinator
Michaela Banks
Ticketing Operations Coordinator
Vanessa Knox
Ticketing Assistants
Georgia Thorne
Jess Macaulay

EXTERNAL RELATIONS AND PHILANTHROPY
Head of External Relations & Philanthropy
Malcolm Moir (from November 2011)

CORPORATE PARTNERSHIPS
(formerly Business Development)
Head of Business Development
Malcolm Moir (to November 2011)
Head of Corporate Partnerships
Sasha Degen (from November 2011)
Corporate Partnership Managers
Kate Armstrong-Smith
Catherine Bowe
Kate Dezarnaulds
Cassandra Kevin
Olivia Wynne (to August 2011)
Corporate Partnerships Coordinator
Jessica Flood

Corporate Partnerships Operations Coordinator
Ben Stern

PRODUCTION
Head of Production
John Bayley
Production Manager
Katie Pack
Catering Manager
Fernando Motti
Production Coordinators
Alycia Bangma
Paul Bearne
Production Assistant
Nicole Lombard
Hospitality Coordinator
Morgan McKinlay
Transport Coordinator
Melissa Hamilton
Crewing Coordinator
Jennie Bradbury
Designers
Mathew McCall
Kate Roberts

DOMAIN STAFF
Domain Manager
Tim Pack
Senior Site Manager
Tom Drury
Site Construction Manager
Peter Craig
Domain Coordinator
Luci Taylor
Electricians
Craig Adamson
Ian Godfrey

FESTIVAL FIRST NIGHT
Producer – Programming
Vernon Guest
Producer – Operations
Margot Natoli
Technical Manager
Mick Jessop
Government & Logistics Manager
Briony Leivers
Programming Coordinators
Clara Iaccarino
Kristal Maher
Logistics Coordinator
Sarah Sebastian
Technical Coordinator
Jack Horton
Marketing & Public Relations
Janet Glover
(Janet Glover PR & Events)
Lyndel Feher (The Fresh Group)

SYDNEY FESTIVAL PARRAMATTA
Producer – Programming
Imogen Semmler
Project Manager
Roger Press
Logistics Assistant
Kim Straatemeier
Marketing & Public Relations
Jacqui Bonner Marketing
+ Management
Lyndel Feher (The Fresh Group)

sydney festival

January 7-29 2012

Babel (words)

'The most fiercely resonant dance theatre of the decade.' The Guardian
Sidi Larbi Cherkaoui /
Damien Jalet / Antony Gormley
Sydney Theatre at Walsh Bay
January 9-11, 13,14

Beautiful Burnout

From the creators of the 2008 Sydney Festival hit, *Black Watch*
Frantic Assembly and
National Theatre of Scotland
York Theatre, Seymour Centre
January 18-22, 24-29

'Tis Pity She's a Whore

A brother and sister's passionate and shocking descent into hell
Cheek by Jowl
Sydney Theatre at Walsh Bay
January 17-21

Assembly

An awe-inspiring mixture of movement and voice
Chunky Move, Victorian Opera and
Sydney Philharmonia Choirs
City Recital Hall Angel Place
January 11-14

Book now Sydney Festival: 1300 668 812
sydneyfestival.org.au

NSW GOVERNMENT

Principal Sponsor

Instant Boiling Water

'THE PLAY IS OFTEN WILDLY FUNNY, SO IMPROBABLE IS THE MIRE OF GREED AND LECHERY, AND YET EVERY LAUGH IS ANOTHER NAIL IN THE COFFIN OF THE COUNCIL'S PROBITY… THIS IS VITAL, ENGAGING THEATRE THAT SERVES AN INVALUABLE FUNCTION IN HELPING TO PURGE THE CANKER.' JOHN SHAND *SMH* 2011

IMAGE: HEIDRUN LÖHR

A VERSION 1.0 AND MERRIGONG THEATRE COMPANY
CO-PRODUCTION PRESENTED BY CARRIAGEWORKS

THE TABLE OF KNOWLEDGE

In February 2008, the Independent Commission Against Corruption began investigating allegations of corruption involving local developers and former staff of Wollongong Council. Exposing sexual obsessions, envelopes full of cash, and a secret cabal of powerful men that met regularly around a plastic table outside a local kebab shop, the resultant scandal culminated with the sacking of the entire Council. Version 1.0 turns its forensic theatrical vision onto this scandal to produce a hilarious and compelling interrogation of power, corruption and good governance in contemporary Australia.

13 – 24 MARCH 2012
TICKETS ON SALE NOW
CARRIAGEWORKS.COM.AU

The Belvoir Story

**One building.
Six hundred people.
Thousands of stories.**

When the Nimrod Theatre building in Belvoir Street, Surry Hills, was threatened with demolition in 1984, more than 600 people – ardent theatre lovers together with arts, entertainment and media professionals – formed a syndicate to buy the building and save this unique performance space in inner-city Sydney.

Over 25 years later, this space, known as Belvoir St Theatre, continues to be the home of one of Australia's most celebrated theatre companies – Belvoir. Under the artistic leadership of Ralph Myers and General Manager Brenna Hobson, Belvoir engages Australia's most prominent and promising playwrights, directors, actors and designers to realise an annual season of work that is dynamic, challenging and visionary. As well as performing at home, Belvoir regularly takes to the road, touring to major arts centres and festivals both nationally and internationally.

Both the Upstairs and Downstairs stages at Belvoir St Theatre have nurtured the talents of many renowned Australian artists: actors including Geoffrey Rush, Cate Blanchett, Catherine McClements, Deb Mailman and Richard Roxburgh; writers such as Tommy Murphy, Jonathan Gavin, Lally Katz and Kate Mulvany; directors including Simon Stone, Benedict Andrews, Wesley Enoch, Rachael Maza and former Belvoir Artistic Director Neil Armfield.

Belvoir's position as one of Australia's most innovative and acclaimed theatre companies has been determined by such landmark productions as *The Diary of a Madman, The Blind Giant is Dancing, Cloudstreet, Measure for Measure, Keating!, Parramatta Girls, Exit the King, The Alchemist, Hamlet, Waiting for Godot, The Sapphires, Who's Afraid of Virginia Woolf?* and *Stuff Happens*.

Belvoir receives government support for its activities from the Federal Government through the Major Performing Arts Board of the Australia Council and the State Government through Arts NSW.

Belvoir Staff

18 Belvoir Street, Surry Hills NSW 2010
Email mail@belvoir.com.au Web www.belvoir.com.au
Administration (02) 9698 3344 Facsimile (02) 9319 3165 Box Office (02) 9699 3444

Artistic Director
Ralph Myers
General Manager
Brenna Hobson

Belvoir Board
Anne Britton
Rob Brookman
Andrew Cameron (Chair)
Peter Carroll
Michael Coleman
Gail Hambly
Brenna Hobson
Frank Macindoe
Ralph Myers

Belvoir St Theatre Board
Trefor Clayton (Chair)
Stuart McCreery
Angela Pearman
Nick Schlieper
Kingsley Slipper

Artistic & Programming
Resident Director
Simon Stone
Associate Director – New Projects
Eamon Flack
Associate Artists
Kylie Farmer
Stefan Gregory
Frank Mainoo
Associate Producer
Tahni Froudist
Literary Manager
Anthea Williams
PlayWriting Australia Resident Playwright
Tommy Murphy
PlayWriting Australia Associate Playwrights
Kit Brookman
Nakkiah Lui
Mei Tsering

Education
Education Manager
Jane May
Education Resources & Regional Access
Cathy Hunt

Administration
Artistic Administrator
John Woodland
Administration Coordinator
Maeve O'Donnell

Finance & Operations
Head of Finance & Operations
Richard Drysdale
Financial Administrator
Ann Brown
Accounts/Payroll Officer
Susan Jack
IT & Operations Manager
Jan S. Goldfeder

Box Office
Box Office Manager
Katinka Van Ingen
Assistant Box Office Managers
Tanya Ginori-Cairns
Alana Hicks

Front of House
Front of House Manager
Ohmeed Ahi
Assistant Front of House Manager
Brooke Louttit

Development
Development Manager
Katy Wood
Partnerships Coordinator
Zoë Hart
Philanthropy Coordinator
Pearl Kermani

Marketing
Marketing Manager
Tina Walsberger
Marketing Coordinator
Marty Jamieson
Publications Coordinator
Gabrielle Bonney
Publicist
Elly Michelle Clough

Production
Production Manager
Chris Mercer
Production Coordinator
Eliza Maunsell
Production Assistant
Rosealee Pearson
Technical Manager
Len Samperi
Resident Stage Manager
Luke McGettigan
Construction Manager
Govinda Webster
Head Mechanist
Damion Holling
Costume Coordinator
Judy Tanner
Downstairs Technical Supervisor
Jack H. Audas Preston

Belvoir Donors

We give our heartfelt thanks to all our donors for their loyal and generous support.

Foundation Donors
Make a significant financial investment in the Belvoir Creative Development Fund.

Neil Armfield AO
Anne Britton
Rob Brookman & Verity Laughton
Andrew Cameron
Janet & Trefor Clayton
Anne & Michael Coleman
Hartley & Sharon Cook
Gail Hambly
Anne Harley
Hal & Linda Herron
Louise Herron & Clark Butler
Victoria Holthouse
Peter & Rosemary Ingle
Ian Learmonth & Julia Pincus
Helen Lynch
Frank Macindoe
Macquarie Group Foundation
David Marr
Ann Sherry & Michael Hogan
Victoria Taylor
Mary Vallentine AO
Kim Williams AM

2011 Chairs Group
Supports the creative development of Indigenous work at Belvoir.

Anonymous 2
Antoinette Albert
Jillian Broadbent AO
Keith & Leslie Bryant
Jan Chapman & Stephen O'Rourke
Louise Christie
Warren Coleman & Therese Kenyon
Kathleen & Danny Gilbert
Girgensohn Foundation
Marion Heathcote & Brian Burfitt
HLA Management Pty Ltd
Belinda Hutchinson AM
The Jarzabek Family
Cassandra Kelly
Hilary Linstead
Cajetan Mula (Honorary Member)
Ross McLean & Fiona Beith
John Morris
A.O. Redmond
Michael Rose & Jo D'Antonio
Ann Sherry AO

Victoria Taylor
Penny Ward
David & Jen Watson
Dr Candice Bruce & Michael Whitworth
Kim Williams AM
Cathy Yuncken

2011/2012 B Keepers
Income received from B Keepers underpins all of our activities.

B Keepers
Anonymous (5)
A & R Maxwell
Robert & Libby Albert
Gil Appleton
Claire Armstrong & John Sharpe
Berg Family Foundation
Bev & Phil Birnbaum
Max Bonnell
Ellen Borda
Anne Britton
Mary Jo & Lloyd Capps
Brian T. Carey
Elaine Chia
Jane Christensen
Louise Christie
Peter Cudlipp & Barbara Schmidt
Suzanne & Michael Daniel
Chris & Bob Ernst
Jeanne Eve
Peter Fay
Peter Graves
David & Kathryn Groves
Sophie Guest
David Haertsch
Wendy & Andrew Hamlin
Beth Harpley
John Head
Marion Heathcote & Brian Burfitt
Michael & Doris Hobbs
Peter & Jessie Ingle
Rosemary & Adam Ingle
Anita Jacoby
The Jarzabek Family
Avril Jeans
Rosemarie & Kevin Jeffers-Palmer
Margaret Johnston
Rob & Corinne Johnston
Phil Kachoyan
Colleen Kane
Antoinette le Marchant

Jennifer Ledgar & Bob Lim
Stephanie Lee
Atul Lele
Hilary Linstead
Prof. Elizabeth More AM
Dr David Nguyen
D & L Parsonage
Timothy & Eva Pascoe
Richard & Heather Rasker
Greg Roger
Geoffrey Rush
Andrew & Louise Sharpe
Peter and Jan Shuttleworth
Edward Simpson
Chris & Bea Sochan
Victoria Taylor
Judy Thomson
Sue Thomson
Brian Thomson & Budi Hernowibowo
Mary Vallentine AO
Alison Wearn
Judy & Sam Weiss
Paul & Jennifer Winch
Iain & Judy Wyatt

Corporate B Keepers
Constructability Recruitment
Macquarie Group Foundation
Sterling Mail Order

Education Donors
Provide opportunities for young people throughout NSW to access our work.

Anonymous (5)
Ian Barnett
Judy Binns
Jan Burnswoods
Rae de Teliga
Jane Diamond
Priscilla Guest
Julie Hannaford
Beth Harpley
Dorothy Hoddinott
Susan Hyde
Peter & Rosemary Ingle
Stewart & Jillian Kellie
Robyn Kremer
Margaret Lederman
Zula Nittim
Patricia Novikoff
Judith Olsen
Martine Robins

Peter & Jan Shuttleworth
Chris & Bea Sochan
The Spence Family
Kerry Stubbs
Jane Westbrook
Zee Yusuf

General Donors over $250

Provide valuable support to the projects most in need throughout the year.

Anonymous (13)
Jes Andersen
Ross & Barb Armfield
Catherine & Chris Baldwin
Alec Brennan
Kim Burton
Andrew Cameron
Michael & Colleen Chesterman
Judy Cole
Dayn Cooper
Timothy and Bryony Cox
Diane Dunlop
Anton Enus & Roger Henning
R.D & P.M Evans
Leon Fink
Valmae Freilich
Frances Garrick
Dr Ronald Lee Gaudreau
Helen Thwaites & Peter Gray
Phillip & Vivien Green
Yoram & Sandra Gross
Priscilla Guest
Juliet Harper
Julie Hannaford
Libby Higgin
Dorothy Hoddinott AO
Despina & Iphygeni Kallinikos
Su Kennedy
Josephine Key
Margaret Lederman
Ross Littlewood & Alexandra Curtin
Heidrun Lohr
Christopher Matthies
David and Barbara Millons
John Morgan
J P Morrison
Jane Munro
Annabelle Andrews & Peter Murray
Dr Peter & June Musgrove
Irena Nebenzahl

Andrew & Toni Noble
Anne O'Driscoll
Judy & Geoff Patterson
Natalie Pelham
Greeba Pritchard
Marguerite Rona
Lesley & Andrew Rosenberg
Mark and Ruth Sampson
Tim & Vivienne Sharpe
Agnes Sinclair
Eileen Slarke and Family
Tim Smyth
Paul Stein
Lee Tanabe
Anthony Tarleton
Chris Vik & Chelsea Albert
Sarah Walters
Lynne Watkins and Nicholas Harding
David Watson
Sam & Judy Weiss
Brian & Patricia Wright
Carolyn Wright

Belvoir is very grateful to accept all donations. Donations over $2 are tax deductible. If you would like to make a donation, or would like further information about any of our donor programs please call our Philanthropy Coordinator Pearl Kermani on 02 8396 6219 or email pearl@belvoir.com.au

List correct at time of printing.

Special Thanks

We would like to acknowledge long-time subscriber Cajetan Mula. Cajetan will always be remembered for his generosity to Belvoir.

Sunday Forum

The bigger picture, the story behind the show, the who's who and the what's what – Sunday Forum is the new window into our work. There'll be a Sunday Forum for every Upstairs show in 2012, at 3pm on the second to last Sunday of the season. Join us in the theatre and we'll have a panel of special guests – performers, creatives, commentators, reviewers, pundits – for a discussion on the show and how it fits into the world at large.

You'll have a chance to ask your burning questions during the forum, and continue the discussion informally with us in the foyer afterwards.

Sunday Forums are free, and you don't need to have seen the show yet to be involved. Each topic will be firmed up once the show opens; check our website or call Box Office for updated information.

See you there!

Bookings are essential and are available four weeks before each forum.
Book: www.belvoir.com.au/sundayforum
or call Box Office on 02 9699 3444.

Buried City
Sunday 29 January

Thyestes
Sunday 12 February
at CarriageWorks

Babyteeth
Sunday 11 March

Every Breath
Sunday 22 April

Strange Interlude
Sunday 10 June

Death of a Salesman
Sunday 5 August

Conversation Piece
Sunday 16 September

Private Lives
Sunday 4 November

Beautiful One Day
Sunday 16 December

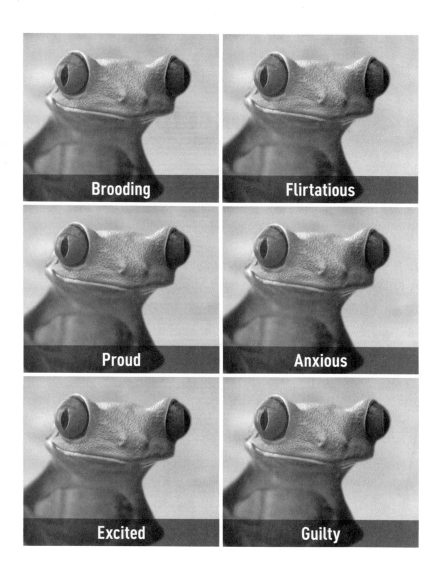

Brooding	Flirtatious
Proud	Anxious
Excited	Guilty

At Optus, we know our role in theatre.

OK, so Optus aren't the world's finest thespians. But we do know how to make theatre possible for everyone, through our special collaboration with Belvoir. Our unique 'Charitable Tickets' and 'Unwaged Performance Programs' offer free tickets to those who rarely have the opportunity to enjoy the theatre.

OPT11094

30% OFF
a 3-day subscription

Get the *Herald* 3-day entertainment package delivered for just **$109**. This 26 week package includes Friday and Saturday's *Sydney Morning Herald* plus *The Sun-Herald*. Saving 30% off the newsstand price.

With Metro, Spectrum and S covering the best of Sydney's cultural life, the *Herald* entertainment package is your definitive guide to what's going on.

Life's Calling

Visit **subscribe.smh.com.au/herald**
or call **13 66 66** and quote HERALD

The Sydney Morning Herald
— NEWSPAPER OF THE YEAR —

For full terms and conditions visit subscribe.smh.com.au/3day

Make your brand centre stage

EYE is a leading Out-of-Home advertising company specialising in roadside billboards, shopping centre, airport and university media.

eyecorp.com
02 8584 2222

EYE is proud to partner with Belvoir

eye

www.bakermckenzie.com

Be inspired

At Ernst & Young we are passionate about our commitment to the Arts. Belvoir provides a fantastic platform for inspiration and Ernst & Young is proud to play a supporting role.

For further information on our Arts sponsorship program, please visit our website:

What's next?
ey.com/au/arts

 ERNST & YOUNG
Quality In Everything We Do

S1022050 SCORE AU00000031
Liability limited by a scheme approved under Professional Standards Legislation.

REGENTS COURT
UNIQUE STYLISH STUDIO ACCOMMODATION

Belvoir's home away from home

For bookings please contact
www.RegentsCourtSydney.com.au
02 9358 1533

VINI
PROUD SUPPORTER OF BELVOIR

3/118 DEVONSHIRE ST (ON HOLT)
SURRY HILLS 9698 5131
TUES - FRI NOON - LATE
SAT 5PM - LATE
WWW.VINI.COM.AU

VINI IS OPEN FOR
PRE-THEATRE DINING & APERITIVO

121BC IS OPEN FOR
POST-THEATRE DINING & DIGESTIVO
WWW.121BC.COM.AU

Opening Act

Cellarmasters
PASSIONATE ABOUT WINE
cellarmasters.com.au

bird cow fish

PRE-THEATRE DINNERS

FROM $45.00 PER PERSON
FOR AN ENTRÉE &
A MAIN COURSE

BIRD COW FISH IS A
LEISURELY WALK TO BELVOIR

PLEASE CALL **02 9380 4090**
TO MAKE YOUR RESERVATION

good simple delicious

Shops 4 & 5, 500 Crown Street Surry Hills

"Think inside the rectangle."

Lisette, Avant Card fan

FREECARD MEDIA

Avant Card is a proud supporter of Belvoir; pick up a free postcard from the foyer.

---

cocktail parties - **dinner parties** - boardroom lunches - **weddings** - conferences

SILVER SPOON
CATERERS

www.silverspoon.net.au - 0418 248 669

 www.facebook.com/silverspooncaterers

would like to thank these generous supporters

Our Principal Supporters

Principal Sponsor

Instant Boiling Water

Leadership Partners

Daily Telegraph
Sunday Telegraph

Strategic Partner

Major Sponsor

Special Distinguished Sponsors

Distinguished Sponsors

Star Sponsors

Contributors
Avant Card
BMF
Cabcharge
Coates Hire
Datalicious
Deepend
Dimmi
Eardrum
ES Group Australia
Flourish Flower Merchants
Icebergs Dining Room and Bar
Motorola Rental Direct
The Nest
Pureprofile
Rolling Stone

Professional Partners
Braithwaite Steiner Pretty
DLA Piper
Hapag-Lloyd AG
Holman Webb
PR Newswire
RDA Research
Woolcott Research

Festival Philanthropy
Sydney Festival launched the Director's Circle, a philanthropic program, for the 2008 Festival. This program has grown from strength to strength, providing supporters with personal insights that come out of a close relationship. Funds generated are of great assistance to the staging of the Festival and are expected to be of increasing importance in the future.

Earlier this year Sydney Festival developed an Associate Producer program to secure specific financial support for *I Am Eora*. This has proved to be a very attractive way for Festival supporters to assist with major new initiatives of the Festival. For information about the Director's Circle or the Associate Producer program please contact Malcolm Moir on 02 8248 6521 or malcolm.moir@sydneyfestival.org.au

Belvoir Sponsors

Corporate Partner

Major Sponsors

Associate Sponsors

Event Sponsors

One Earth Foods
Silver Spoon Caterers

Supporters

Indigenous Theatre at Belvoir supported by The Balnaves Foundation

CITY OF SYDNEY

Besen Family Foundation
Coca-Cola Australia Foundation
Enid Irwin Charitable Trust managed by Perpetual
Gandevia Foundation
The Greatorex Foundation
Media Tree
Teen Spirit Charitable Foundation managed by Perpetual
Thomas Creative
Vincent Fairfax Family Foundation

Government Partners

For more information on partnership opportunities please contact our Development Manager Katy Wood on 02 8396 6224 or email katy@belvoir.com.au

www.currency.com.au

Visit Currency Press' website now to:
- Buy your books online
- Browse through our full list of titles, from plays to screenplays, books on theatre, film and music, and more
- Choose a play for your school or amateur performance group by cast size and gender
- Obtain information about performance rights
- Find out about theatre productions and other performing arts news across Australia
- For students, read our study guides
- For teachers, access syllabus and other relevant information
- Sign up for our email newsletter

The performing arts publisher